75 Hikes in™
NEW MEXICO

75 Hikes in™
NEW MEXICO

Craig Martin

THE
MOUNTAINEERS

For June, my favorite hiking companion

 Published by
The Mountaineers
1001 SW Klickitat Way, Suite 201
Seattle, Washington 98134

9 8 7 6 5
5 4 3 2 1

Published simultaneously in Canada by Douglas & McIntyre, Ltd., 1615 Venables Street, Vancouver, B.C. V5L 2H1

Published simultaneously in Great Britain by Cordee, 3a DeMontfort Street, Leicester, England, LE1 7HD

Manufactured in the United States of America

Edited by Paula Thurman
Maps by Craig Martin
All photographs by author except as noted
Cover design by The Mountaineers Books
Book design and typography by The Mountaineers Books
Book layout by Word Graphics

Cover photograph: *Chaco Canyon, New Mexico* © Randy Wells/Tony Stone Images
Frontispiece: *Heart Lake with July snow on Latir Mesa*

Library of Congress Cataloging-in-Publication Data
Martin, Craig, 1952–
  75 hikes in New Mexico / Craig Martin.
     p.   cm.
  Includes bibliographical references (p.   ) and index.
  ISBN 0-89886-441-0
  1. Hiking—New Mexico—Guidebooks. 2. New Mexico—Guidebooks.
I. Title.
GV199.42.N6M37   1995
796.5'1'09789—dc20   95–34994
                                                              CIP

CONTENTS

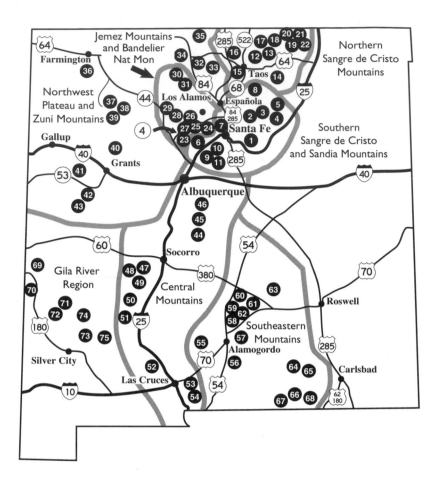

On the trail in Sawmill Meadow (June Fabryka-Martin photo)

south, these conditions can last until early November. Fall hikers should always know the current weather forecast before starting on a trip. Blustery, fast-moving cold fronts can bring heavy snow to the northern mountains as early as mid-September, although these storms usually wait until mid-October. Each fall, search-and-rescue teams are kept busy by hikers who head unprepared into the backcountry regardless of the forecast.

Mountain trails in the north are closed by snow by late October or mid-November. In the south, mountain trails are often open until December but desert hikes are possible throughout the winter, except when surprisingly cold storms bring wind and snowy conditions for a day or two at a time. Always know the latest weather forecast before any winter trip.

Colorado columbine

LIGHTNING AND FLASH FLOODS

Open spaces are no place in which to be caught during a summer thunderstorm: New Mexico ranks second in the nation in number of lightning-caused deaths per year. Plan to be off ridges and peaks before noon. Storms build rapidly, and hikers need to be constantly vigilant of the weather. When caught by an unexpected storm, stay off ridgelines and open mesa tops and keep out of meadows and away from lone trees or rocks. Seek safety in low ground, in extensive forested areas, or in large caves. When no shelter is available, avoid small caves and shallow depressions. Stow backpacks and other metal objects at least 30 feet away and use clothing to insulate yourself from the ground. Squat on two feet and keep as low a profile as possible.

A great paradox of hiking in the dry Southwest is the serious threat posed by running water. Precipitation may be rare in the desert, but summer storms can nonetheless produce inordinate amounts of rain in a short time. Water quickly collects in drainages, turning a dry stream bed into a raging torrent within minutes. Stay out of dry washes and arroyos during storms, and never set up camp in a dry watercourse. Be aware that a storm in the upper portion of a drainage can send a wall of water down to a sunny, lower portion, so keep an eye on the surrounding

weather. Do not try to ford streams filled with flood water. Be patient—
high flow rates usually subside in a few hours.

IMPORTANCE OF WATER

Along with sunny skies comes a dry climate where water is precious
to all living things. Hikers will lose water to temperature regulation,
increased respiration, and increased metabolic rates. By the time a
hiker feels thirsty, he or she is already a quart low on fluids. Maintain-
ing body fluid balance is a critical part of hiking in New Mexico.

Excessive fluid loss can lead to heat exhaustion, a potentially serious condition, for which symptoms include reduced perspiration, rapid
pulse, dizziness, and general weakness. Hikers with any of these signs
should get out of the sun and drink large quantities of water. Without
careful attention, heat exhaustion can lead to heat stroke, a much
more dangerous condition characterized by no perspiration, hot skin,
and a high body temperature. These signs indicate a medical emergency requiring urgent attention. First aid is an immediate reduction
of body temperature by moving to a cool location, increased fluid
intake, and cool compresses to the skin.

Heat-related medical problems can be avoided by drinking plenty of
water before starting out on a hike and then drinking regularly during
the trip. Plan on at least a half-gallon of fluid per person for a day hike
and a gallon per person per day for an overnight trip.

PROTECTION FROM THE SUN

The near-constant blue skies of the high desert are no myth, but
there is a price to pay. Skin cancer rates are high in the Southwest,
and visitors and natives alike must take precautions against too much
of a good thing. Summer and winter, hikers must protect themselves
from the sun.

The best protection is a long-sleeved shirt and long pants, even in
summer. Light colors will help reflect the intense summer sun, and a
loose fit will help keep hikers cool. Wide-brimmed hats are standard
equipment all year long. Additional protection for the eyes is provided
by high quality sunglasses that screen at least ninety-five percent of
ultraviolet radiation.

In addition to protective clothing, hikers should use copious sunscreen. Apply an SFP 15 or higher formula at least every four hours.
Sweatproof types of sunscreen now available stay on well during
exercise. For full protection, coat hands, neck, face, and ears.

ELEVATION FACTORS

Many mountain trails in New Mexico lead to elevations above 8,000
feet. Out-of-state hikers unaccustomed to altitude should avoid problems with high elevations by allowing at least 2 days to acclimate at a
mid-range elevation before attempting a hike above 9,000 feet. Thin
air increases exertion and visitors should slow down to a comfortable
pace, which may be considerably slower than their normal hiking
speed. Quick ascents above 10,000 feet can lead to a variety of medical

problems, such as mountain sickness. Symptoms include headache, nausea, weakness, and general achiness. Problems usually disappear with a return to lower elevations, but if symptoms persist, medical attention is required.

CRITTER COMPLICATIONS

Eight species of rattlesnake reside within the borders of New Mexico, and at least one type is found in all habitats ranging from lowland deserts to conifer forest. In the north, most rattlesnakes are found below 7,000 feet, but they are occasionally spotted up to 9,000 feet. Rattlesnakes are common at all elevations in the southern part of the state up to 10,000 feet.

Rattlers hibernate during the winter months and into May in the north. In summer, they avoid hot sunshine and are generally found at night. Caution is advised when hiking at dusk or at night, and using a flashlight is recommended. Rattlers are most active in the daytime during spring and fall. Snakes will be found sunning on ledges or in the partial shade of trees. Hikers can avoid rattlesnakes by staying on the trail and always watching their footing. Most bites occur below the knee, and high-top boots and long pants afford some protection from

Beaver lodge

snakes. Off the trail, never place your hand on a ledge above your head. Most bites occur from people handling rattlesnakes. The buzzing rattle of the snakes is an effective warning of their presence, although many a hiker has unknowingly stepped directly over rattlers hidden behind rocks or logs in the trail.

Although the once-common grizzly bear is no longer found here, black bears are common inhabitants of all forested mountain ranges in New Mexico. Bear encounters are infrequent, but increase during dry summers. A bear spotted along a trail will usually turn tail and be quickly gone. Hikers who encounter a bear should make the bear aware of their presence by talking in conversational tones and make certain not to get between a mother and her cubs. In camp, although it is usually not necessary, it is good practice to tie food in a tree at least 10 feet off the ground and out of reach of the trunk. If a bear does get food or equipment, do not attempt to take it away.

Scorpions range throughout New Mexico and are most common in the southern half of the state. New Mexican species are not deadly and have stings similar to that of bees. Scorpions hide under rocks and tree bark during the day, coming out at night to prey on insects. Their secretive habits make them easy to avoid; most hikers will never see one. Because scorpions seek damp, dark places, it is, however, a good idea for backpackers to shake out clothing and check shoes and boots before putting them on in the morning.

Bothersome insects are pleasantly absent from most parts of New Mexico, but two kinds of arthropods found here carry serious diseases and should be avoided. Tall grasses are home to ticks, which are most abundant in spring and early summer. Although Lyme disease has not yet been found to originate in New Mexico, it may arrive soon. Ticks do carry Rocky Mountain spotted fever and Colorado tick fever. Symptoms for both are flu-like. Check for ticks after each trip. If any are found, remove them with tweezers, and for several weeks, watch for signs of illness.

More serious in nature is the presence of plague. This life-threatening disease is carried by fleas living on host animals. Thus, it is important to avoid contact with wild animals, particularly members of the rodent family, dead or alive. Camp away from animal burrows. After an outdoor trip in New Mexico, anyone with high fever and swelling in the armpits and groin, particularly visitors who are back at home, should alert physicians to the possibility of plague.

The latest addition to the list of life-threatening diseases in New Mexico is hantavirus, a serious respiratory illness. Humans contract this disease by inhaling dry mouse urine, particularly that of the common deer mouse. Flu-like symptoms—fever, headache, and cough—are followed by a rapid increase of fluid in the lungs. Half of all cases end in death. Avoid hantavirus by avoiding mice. Backpackers should use a tent with a floor and pitch it away from rodent burrows. Store food in sealed containers off the ground.

What to Bring Along

The difference between an enjoyable outdoor excursion and disaster is often preparation. Careful planning for all hikes, no matter what distance, is important for the safety of all hikers. An excellent starting place for loading a pack is the list of the Ten Essentials from The Mountaineers.

1. Extra clothing
2. Extra food
3. Sun protection
4. Pocketknife
5. Firestarter candle or chemical fuel
6. First-aid kit and snakebite kit
7. Matches in a waterproof container
8. Flashlight
9. Map
10. Compass

CLOTHING

Hikers in New Mexico are likely to encounter a wide range of temperatures during the course of a day. To meet the challenges of weather, always dress in layers. In cool spring and fall, begin with a zipper-neck shirt made from synthetic material, then wear a moisture-absorbing cotton layer on top. Synthetic-material tights or nylon pants are also suitable for this time of year. For an insulating layer, a light- or mid-weight fleece jacket or pullover is an excellent choice. When it is colder, fleece pants are warm and offer good protection even when wet.

Proper dress is important in summer, too, when low temperatures and rain or even snow are always possible at high elevations. Wear a long-sleeved shirt and pants of light cotton. For an overnight trip, add a light fleece jacket and pants. Carry extra warm clothing, even in July and August.

In all seasons, carry rain gear. Getting wet is the most serious threat to backcountry hikers, because a drenching from a storm can quickly lead to hypothermia. Anticipate summer showers every afternoon by carrying a rain jacket and pants. Waterproof outer layers are even more important in spring and fall when temperatures can quickly drop to dangerous levels.

Footgear is an important part of hiking equipment. Sturdy, light-weight boots are best for comfort and help reduce erosion to the trail. Because of the dry climate, light-duty boots with fabric and leather uppers are adequate for much of the hiking in New Mexico. These are generally a few ounces lighter and are cooler than other boots, but they often lack good waterproofing. For mountain hiking, especially during the summer rainy season, waterproof boots with full leather or synthetic uppers are recommended. Heavy boots also offer additional protection on rough, rocky trails. Proper socks can also add to comfort. A

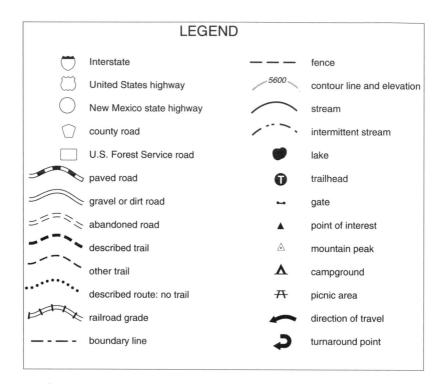

LEGEND

Interstate		fence	
United States highway		contour line and elevation	5600
New Mexico state highway		stream	
county road		intermittent stream	
U.S. Forest Service road		lake	
paved road		trailhead	
gravel or dirt road		gate	
abandoned road		point of interest	
described trail		mountain peak	
other trail		campground	
described route: no trail		picnic area	
railroad grade		direction of travel	
boundary line		turnaround point	

combination of thin liner socks with thicker synthetic or wool padded outer socks works best.

MAPS

A good state map will lead to the vicinity of the trailhead. Pick one up at one of the tourist information centers around the state, or call the New Mexico Tourism Division at 1-800-545-2040. Maps of the state's seven national forests will be helpful in locating most trailheads and are available for a moderate fee from the Forest Supervisor offices listed at the end of this book.

The outline maps included with each hike are meant as general guides and should not take the place of large-scale maps, particularly for the longer hikes into the backcountry. Nothing can substitute for the most recent United States Geological Survey (USGS) 7.5-minute quadrangle maps. The maps required for each hike are listed in the summary table. Topographic maps are available at many outdoor outfitters around the state and directly from the USGS at Western Distribution Branch, Box 25286, Federal Center Building 41, Denver, CO 80225.

WATER

The importance of water to hikers in New Mexico cannot be overstated. Low humidity, high temperature, and high elevation combine to create conditions that require hikers to carry at least a half gallon of water per person for a day hike and at least a gallon per person per day for an overnight trip. Always keep an emergency supply of water in the support vehicle.

Hikers should bring all the water they need on day trips, but carrying sufficient water for an extended stay in the mountains is difficult. Plan to camp near water. All water taken from backcountry sources must be treated before use. Cattle often graze in the backcountry and share water sources with hikers. Giardia, a protozoan parasite that causes an unpleasant and potentially serious intestinal disorder, is present throughout the state.

The safest method of treating water is to boil it vigorously for 10 minutes. Because water boils at a lower temperature at high altitude, boiling time must be increased above 7,000 feet. Chemical treatment with chlorine or hyperiodide tablets is an easy method of water treatment. Mechanical filters can treat large volumes of water in a short time, but they vary in their efficiency. For the safest results, use a filter with a 0.02-micron screen.

Standing outer wall of Tsin Kletsin

Yellow daisies growing from beneath rocks

Responsible Hiking

PRIVATE LAND

Complicated land ownership laws dating back to the days of Spanish rule and the abundance of mining claims have left New Mexico checkered with pockets of private land within public use areas. As a result, ten of the hikes in this book pass through private land and many other trips pass close to private property. *To avoid problems with land-owners, note the boundaries of public land on the hike maps and obey all No Trespassing signs.*

Six hikes cross private land on public easements negotiated by the Forest Service or the Bureau of Land Management: Atalaya Mountain (No. l), La Bajada Hill (No. 6), Lobo Peak (No. 12), Broad Canyon (No. 52), Willie White Canyon (No. 57), and Devils Den (No. 67). In addition, two hikes require crossing private land to access the trailhead: South Sandia Peak (No. 11) and Frisco Box (No. 69). In each case, hikers are permitted to cross private land on the trail or road. Do not stray from the designated pathway, and leave all gates as they are found. These easements are the result of generosity of the landowners and their continuance is dependent upon the courteous and respectful use by hikers. Landowners may close down access through their property at any time. Before starting out on one of these hikes, check with the managing agency on the current status of the easement.

For the Kitchen Mesa (No. 32) and Mesa Montosa (No. 33) trips, permission to hike must be obtained at the Ghost Ranch Office, as detailed in the hike descriptions.

MINIMUM IMPACT USE

Before the explosion of wilderness use over the last 30 years, hikers gave little thought to what they did or left behind in the backcountry. But with increasing numbers of wilderness users, it has become necessary for each hiker to consider the impact his or her trip has on the trail, the environment, and other trail users. Current thinking is best expressed by the phrase "leave no trace." All hikers should carefully plan how they can minimize their impact on the outdoors while still having an enjoyable wilderness experience.

Minimum impact use goes far beyond common sense. All hikers should carefully study the ways they can become clean users of the backcountry and develop an attitude that every user shares the responsibility to leave the wilderness in its pristine condition. The following suggestions are based on Leave No Trace materials developed by the National Outdoor Leadership School, the Bureau of Land Management, the National Park Service, and the United States Forest Service.

At Home

Minimum impact hiking begins at home with careful planning. A well-thought-out trip reduces the potential for a damaging and costly search-and-rescue operation. Carry a map and compass, and know how to use them to stay on the planned route as well as how to determine location when lost. Before leaving on a trip, hikers should leave a detailed itinerary of their trip with a knowledgable friend. Also, reduce waste before hiking by repacking food in reusable containers that will not be inadvertently left behind.

On the Trail

When hiking, be considerate of other trail users. Hike quietly, and rest off the trail on rocks or other durable surfaces that will not show signs of trampling.

Trails and the surrounding terrain can be easily damaged. On established trails, hike single file to avoid widening the tread. On muddy stretches of trail, hike in the established tread to avoid creating new tracks. Do not short cut switchbacks, a practice that leads quickly to severe trail erosion. When hiking routes with no established trail, hike abreast to avoid repetitive trampling of vegetation and step on rock or sand when possible.

In Camp

Select a campsite with distinct signs of use or in an area that will not be damaged. Sites should be at least 200 feet from water and trails, with the distance increased to a minimum of 300 feet in deserts. In river canyons, camp on sandy beaches or gravel bars below the high water line. The best campsites are also away from and out of view of other campers.

Most packaging material will not burn completely, so pack out all trash and all uneaten food. Buried food will soon be discovered and excavated by animals, increasing their dependence on unnatural food sources.

Calypso orchid

Minimize the impact of camp-fires by cooking with a back-packing stove. When building a campfire, use existing fire rings or a metal firepan and burn only small-diameter dead and down wood. Before leaving, make certain the fire is out, then remove the cold ashes from the ring and scatter them away from camp. Dry washes and sand or gravel stream banks below the high water line make good locations for pit fires. To remove signs of a pit fire, scatter the remains, then fill in the hole. In desert areas, the small amount of dead wood is important to the eco-system and should not be used for fires. Carry in all firewood or go without.

Human waste is best disposed in a "cat" hole at least 6 inches deep placed at least 200 feet from camp and the nearest water. After use, cover the hole with natural materials. Do not bury toilet paper with the waste; pack it out. When cleaning cook-ing utensils, use only a small amount of biodegradable soap. Remove and pack out food particles. Dishwater should be broadcast over a wide area away from camp and water sources. In desert areas, hikers should increase the distance of all waste to water sources to 300 feet.

In narrow river canyons, special precautions must be taken. In silty rivers with large flow volumes, urine and waste water can be dumped into the flow, allowing the large volume to dilute the waste. In moun-tain canyons with low flows, urinate on the banks below the high water line to allow some filtration before the waste reaches the clear stream. Human waste should be packed out of narrow canyons or left in holes well away from the main or side streams.

For more detailed information on how to reduce user impacts on the wilderness, contact Leave No Trace at 1-800-332-4100.

Selecting a Hike

This book holds an eclectic collection of hikes. Trips in several cat-egories were selected. Hikes judged to be New Mexico classics—ones that most hikers who live in or visit the state will want take—are of course included. The climb to the summit of Wheeler Peak is one such classic; the blazing reds of autumn in Fourth of July Canyon and the shimmering dunes at White Sands are other examples. A large number of hikes in out-of-the-way places that see few visitors are also included. Trips to Valle Vidal, Sawmill Meadow, Navajo Peak, Three Rivers Canyon, Vicks Peak, and many others fall into this category. Other locations are little-known and deserve recognition, such as the Three Rivers Petroglyph Site, the Rim Vista Trail, and the Cruces Basin Wilderness. Personal favorites of mine are hikes with a special historic or natural history focus. Hikers on La Bajada and Barranca hills, in Chaco Canyon, on the Catwalk, and Cerro Americano will find a wealth of historic or geologic features that make these true explorations rather than simple hikes.

In most instances, hikers will find clusters of three or more hikes listed for a given mountain range or canyon. The clusters were designed to provide a full weekend of hiking opportunities with a minimal amount of driving.

Throughout this book, five abbreviations are used in connection with roads. Interstate highways are designated with I, United States highways with US, New Mexico state roads with NM, county roads with CR, and Forest Service roads with FR.

Use the summary table at the beginning of each hike description to honestly select a hike suited to your skills. Hikers unaccustomed to walking at elevation should look carefully at the hike distance and elevation gain. Visitors should wait several days before tackling trips over 8 miles long or with more than 2,000 feet of elevation gain.

The summary table for each hike provides the following information:

Managed by: The landowner or managing agency for each hike, who to contact for more or up-to-date information. A list of addresses and telephone numbers is found at the end of the hike descriptions.

Distance: Unless otherwise noted, the distance given is for a round trip. Hike distances were estimated from field data, information provided by the managing agency, and from careful measurement on topographic maps. This method has its shortcomings, and hikers may find distances are as much as twenty percent in error.

Elevation Range: The highest and lowest points of the hike.

Elevation Gain: The cumulative elevation gain for the route as described, including all ascents, as determined with a recording altimeter.

Difficulty: A subjective evaluation of each hike, biased toward casual hikers and those unaccustomed to elevation.

Seasons: The best time of the year to take each hike, based on an average year, which rarely occurs. The weather in New Mexico is notoriously variable, and hikers should always consult the latest weather forecast before starting out on a trip.

Water: The location of potential drinking water along the route. When possible, hikers should carry enough water for the entire hike and not depend on nature to provide a safe and adequate supply. Remember that all water should be treated before use.

Maps: The best available maps for the hike.

Interesting features: The attractions that make each hike worthy of the reader's attention.

A Note About Safety

Safety is an important concern in all outdoor activities. No guidebook can alert you to every hazard or anticipate the limitations of every reader. Therefore, the descriptions of roads, trails, routes, and natural features in this book are not representations that a particular place or excursion will be safe for your party. When you follow any of the routes described in this book, you assume responsibility for your own safety. Under normal conditions, such excursions require the usual attention to traffic, road and trail conditions, weather, terrain, the capabilities of your party, and other factors. Keeping informed on current conditions and exercising common sense are the keys to a safe, enjoyable outing.

The Mountaineers

Hiking in New Mexico is filled with surprises.

Southern Sangre de Cristo and Sandia Mountains

Cañada Ancha as it flows into Caja del Rio Canyon

1 ATALAYA MOUNTAIN

Managed by: Santa Fe National Forest, Española Ranger District
Distance: 9 miles, day hike
Elevation range: 7,300 to 9,100 feet
Elevation gain: 1,800 feet
Difficulty: moderate
Seasons: April to November
Water: carry water
Map: USGS Santa Fe 7.5' quadrangle
Interesting features: views of Santa Fe, trailhead close to town

A climb to the top of Atalaya Mountain on the outskirts of Santa Fe provides hikers with a unique view of the old city. The steep but pleasant trail leads through shady conifer forest to the summit where Santa Fe, with its historic plaza and sprawling new growth, spreads out below. A couple hours on this trail can be a welcome relief from the usual tourist fare in Santa Fe. Be watchful on weekends when this trail may receive moderate use by mountain bikers.

To reach the trailhead from the intersection of Cerrillos Road and St. Francis Drive, go south on St. Francis 0.2 mile and turn left onto Cordova Road. Continue 1.5 miles past Old Pecos Trail, where the name of Cordova Road changes to Armenta Street. At a T intersection, turn left onto Camino Corrales. Cross Old Santa Fe Trail, then bear right onto Garcia Street. At another T intersection, turn right onto Camino del Monte Sol. Almost immediately, turn left onto Camino de Cruz Blanca, which is signed for St. Johns College. Turn right at the entrance to St. Johns in 0.6 mile and park in the lot near the entrance at the signs marking the Atalaya Mountain Trailhead.

Walk east as Trail No. 174 winds through junipers along the edge of a large arroyo. After dropping into the arroyo, watch for signs marking the trail, which soon exits the east (left) side of the stream bed and enters a narrow side canyon. The winding path leads through private

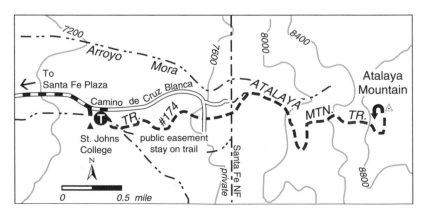

Mushrooms growing in the lush forest of the Sangre de Cristos

land; stay on the trail in this section. At mile 0.9, cross a road and continue straight. On top of a low ridge at mile 1.4, intersect Trail No. 170, an alternate branch of the Atalaya Mountain Trail. Bear right onto a wider trail as it contours around the southwest slope of a ridge through tall ponderosa pines.

After reaching the nose of a spur ridge, the trail swings left and begins to climb. Grades are steep from here to the summit of Atalaya Mountain, which is visible to the right. Where an old, deeply eroded route continues steeply straight ahead, turn right onto a more gentle, but still steep, trail. Climb across a steep slope to reach the ridgeline at mile 2.5. Turn left and continue 0.4 mile to the summit where a reward of fine views of the city of Santa Fe and the Jemez Mountains awaits. After enjoying the view, turn around and descend by the same route.

2 ASPEN RANCH LOOP

Managed by: Santa Fe National Forest, Española Ranger District
Distance: 8 miles, day hike or backpack
Elevation range: 8,900 to 10,200 feet
Elevation gain: 1,600 feet
Difficulty: moderate
Seasons: late May to mid-October
Water: Rio en Medio
Map: USGS Aspen Basin 7.5' quadrangle
Interesting features: high country scenery, fall aspens, picturesque stream

The Aspen Ranch Loop is a scenic hike through the high country of the Sangre de Cristos near Santa Fe. The trip offers miles of pleasant

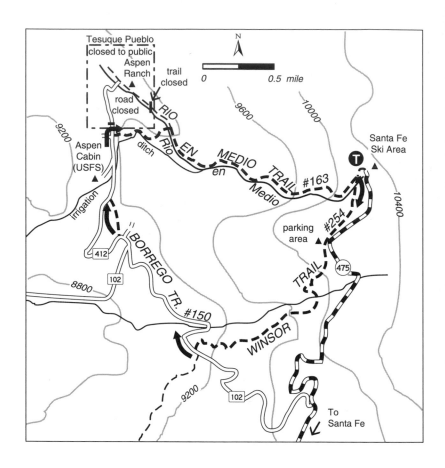

walking on shaded slopes, views of large aspen stands, and a steep climb along a cascading stream. On a smaller scale, hikers will find thousands of summer wildflowers along the route as well as intricate swirling patterns in the banded gneiss at trailside. Take along a fishing rod and try for some of the small trout found in the deep pools of the Rio en Medio. These trails are uncrowded, but on weekends, watch out for mountain bikes on the Winsor Trail segment of the loop.

From Santa Fe, take Washington Avenue north from Paseo de Peralta 0.1 mile to Artist Road, NM 475. Turn right and head toward the Santa Fe Ski Area. Continue about 14 miles to the parking area at the ski basin. Park at the Winsor Trailhead at the northwest corner of the lot.

Begin walking on the Winsor Trail. Immediately cross a bridge and turn left to parallel a small stream. In 0.2 mile, pass through a fence and continue to descend to the intersection with the Rio en Medio Trail No. 163. Turn left to stay on the Winsor Trail; the loop returns to this point at the end of the hike via the Rio en Medio Trail. The Winsor

Trail crosses the Rio en Medio, then crosses several smaller, usually dry drainages as it heads southwest. About a mile from the start, the Winsor Trail reaches a parking area and cross-country ski trail along NM 475. Cross the parking area and pick up the Winsor Trail at a small sign near the road, then descend a series of switchbacks. After crossing a small drainage, begin a long, pleasant stroll as the trail contours along the side of a large canyon. At mile 2.2, reach the top of eight gentle, descending switchbacks. At the bottom, intersect FR 102, which is designated here as the Borrego Trail No. 150. Turn right and walk the dirt road, heading downhill. Continue on the road through the conifer forest for 1.3 miles to the intersection with FR 412. Turn right and walk north on FR 412. In a hundred yards, pass a dirt double track heading north. Continue to the next bend on FR 412, then leave the road on the unmarked Borrego Trail No. 150 as it climbs steeply on the west side of a small dry drainage.

At the top of the hill at mile 4.5, rejoin FR 412 and continue north. Cross an irrigation ditch and enter a small meadow. As the road begins to descend toward a gate at the boundary of Tesuque Pueblo land, pass a new parking area in a small meadow. Pick up the recently rerouted Rio en Medio Trail No. 163 as it climbs steeply up a hill, parallel to a fence, heading east. The trail follows an irrigation ditch to the north and east, crossing over to the slopes above the Rio en Medio. At mile 5.2, the trail cuts away from the ditch and drops steeply down the slope through a wonderful open stand of aspen. At the bottom of the hill, the trail crosses the Rio en Medio and a few small campsites are found nearby. Turn right and climb on the wide trail parallel to the stream. The trail soon enters a narrow stretch of canyon where the trail, perched above the delightful stream, is steep and rocky.

Intricate folds in banded gneiss along the Rio en Medio

At mile 6, the climb moderates. In another mile, enter a large, wet meadow. The trace of the trail disappears in the wet grasses. Head uphill, bearing slightly away from the stream. At the far end of the meadow, the trail leaves the Rio en Medio, enters the forest, and briefly follows a small side stream. After crossing the stream, the trail rejoins the Rio en Medio and briefly becomes very steep. At the top of the hill, again meet the Winsor Trail. Turn left and backtrack 0.3 mile to the trailhead.

3   SPIRIT LAKE

Managed by: Santa Fe National Forest, Pecos Wilderness, Española Ranger District
Distance: 12 miles, day hike or backpack
Elevation range: 10,400 to 11,100 feet
Elevation gain: 2,300 feet
Difficulty: difficult
Seasons: late June to early October
Water: Rio Nambe, Spirit Lake
Maps: Aspen Basin and Cowles USGS 7.5' quadrangles, USFS Pecos Wilderness
Interesting features: high country lake, mountain scenery, fall aspens

The climb to Spirit Lake is a summer getaway from the tourist crowds in Santa Fe, but on weekends the Winsor Trail receives heavy use by hikers. The views from the trail are among the best in the southern Sangre de Cristos and encompass the Jemez Mountains, the Rio Grande Valley, and a close-up look at Santa Fe Baldy. Fall colors are spectacular in this part of the range, making this a popular hike in

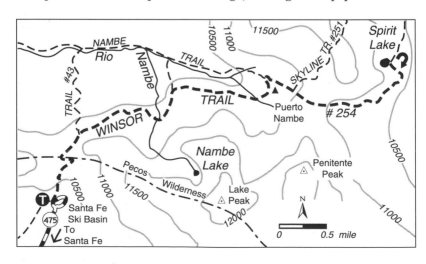

late September. Spirit Lake itself holds rainbow and cutthroat trout, so take along a fishing rod. A few campsites are found in the woods surrounding the lake, but regulations require campsites to be more than 200 feet from the water.

From the plaza in Santa Fe, take Washington Road 0.5 mile north to Artist Road, NM 475, which is signed for the Santa Fe Ski Basin. Turn right and continue 14 miles to the lower parking area at the ski basin. Park near a sign for the Winsor Trail.

Begin hiking on the Winsor Trail No. 254, immediately crossing a bridge and turning right. The first 0.5 mile of trail climbs 500 feet on several graded switchbacks, and is the steepest climb of the trip. At the top of the ridge, cross a fence into the Pecos Wilderness. A stop here for a breather may attract a flock of gray jays tame enough to eat peanuts from an outstretched hand.

Bull elephant's head

A long, pleasant stretch of trail drops gradually on a steep slope high above the Rio Nambe through a deep fir forest dotted with aspen. The deeply shaded north slope can hold snow into late June. At mile 1.2, pass Trail No. 43 dropping steeply to the left. Cross the headwaters of the Rio Nambe at mile 2.2 and follow the trail as it contours to the northeast. As Santa Fe Baldy comes into view, the trail swings east, passing through small meadows of summer wildflowers. Cross another stream at mile 3.3, then climb the next ridge on gentle switchbacks to reach Puerto Nambe, a broad saddle between Santa Fe Baldy and Penitente Peak, at mile 4.

Again heading east, walk through the splendid meadows atop the broad saddle, with Santa Fe Baldy to the left and Penitente Peak to the right. Pass the junction with the Skyline Trail No. 251 to the left and continue straight on the Winsor Trail. Hike single file to prevent further development of parallel tracks across the meadow. The trail drops slowly from the east side of the saddle, traversing a forested south-facing slope. A mile from the saddle, cross a short spur ridge, then drop more sharply to the lake basin. Enjoy the shade of the huge firs surrounding Spirit Lake. The trail's gentle grades make the return trip easier than expected.

4   HAMILTON MESA

Managed by: Santa Fe National Forest, Pecos Wilderness, Pecos Ranger District
Distance: 6 miles, day hike
Elevation range: 9,300 to 10,300 feet
Elevation gain: 1,000 feet
Difficulty: easy
Seasons: late May to late October
Water: carry water
Maps: USGS Elk Mountain 7.5' quadrangle, USFS Pecos Wilderness
Interesting features: wonderful views, mesa-top meadows

The Pecos Wilderness is New Mexico's second-largest and most popular wilderness area. Hamilton Mesa is a long ridge that splits the central Pecos Wilderness in two. From the grassy meadows on the mesa top, the canyon of the Pecos River drops off to the west and that of the Rio Mora to the east. The view from the summit is thus unobstructed in all directions and encompasses all of the highest peaks of the southern Sangre de Cristo Mountains. The view is particularly lovely in the fall when aspens on the surrounding slopes blaze golden yellow.

From Santa Fe, take I 25 to exit 299 at Glorieta. Turn left to cross over the interstate, then turn right on NM 50 for 6 miles to the intersection with NM 63. Turn left and travel up the canyon of the Pecos River. Beyond the Terrero Store, the road has a gravel surface. Bear right onto FR 223, which is signed for Iron Gate Campground about 18 miles from NM 50. Go 4.3 bumpy and winding miles (it only seems like ten) to Iron Gate Campground and park at the trailhead.

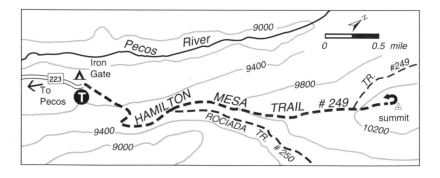

A tall rock cairn marks the summit of Hamilton Mesa.

Begin on the Hamilton Mesa Trail No. 249, walking a single switchback that leads to the top of the ridge about 0.5 mile from the start. On the top, the trail turns left and parallels the ridge. In a grove of aspen trees, look for elk tooth marks on the bark of the trunks. At mile 1.5, reach the intersection with the Rociada Trail No. 250. The Rociada Trail bears right to drop to Mora Flats (see hike No. 5); take the left fork to Hamilton Mesa.

Begin a steeper climb along the flanks of the mesa, first through a small oak thicket, then into a Douglas-fir forest. Two miles from the start, pass through a gate in a large wooden fence and enter an open aspen stand. After entering a meadow, the trail continues to climb, opening increasingly impressive vistas. The highest peaks of the range—Pecos Baldy, Santa Fe Baldy, and Lake Peak—rise to the west. After the trail passes a large, spreading aspen tree, Trail No. 249 bears left. Continue straight on an unmaintained side trail that climbs up a knoll. Follow the trail as it heads toward a gap in a small patch of forest that splits the meadow in two. Walk through the break in the forest, continuing on the trail as it heads to the very summit of Hamilton Mesa.

At mile 3.1, the trail skirts the summit. Leave the trail and finish the final hundred yards cross country, ending at a tall rock cairn. Enjoy the view, then return to the trailhead by the same route.

5 MORA FLATS

Managed by: Santa Fe National Forest, Pecos Wilderness, Pecos Ranger District
Distance: 8 miles, day hike or backpack
Elevation range: 9,200 to 9,500 feet
Elevation gain: 800 feet
Difficulty: easy
Seasons: late May through late October
Water: Rio Mora
Maps: USGS Elk Mountain 7.5' quadrangle, USFS Pecos Wilderness
Interesting Features: huge wildflower-studded meadow, trout fishing, easy access to camping spots

Mora Flats is a huge valley split by several picturesque mountain streams. It makes an easy destination for an overnight trip into the Pecos Wilderness suitable for beginning backpackers or families. The grades are easy, the views spectacular, the fishing excellent, and camp spots are plentiful in the flats. From a base camp, one can day hike several trails to high divides or just fly-fish for small trout in the Rio Mora or the Rio Valdez. Hikers must camp more than 200 feet from the streams.

A good two-day trip can be made by joining this hike with the Hamilton Mesa Trail. Hike to Mora Flats, then, at the junction with the Rio Valdez Trail No. 224, bear left and travel 2 miles upstream, passing several nice campsites along the way. At the junction with Trail No. 270, turn left (west) and climb over Hamilton Mesa to Trail No. 249. Turn left (south) and follow the trail back to Iron Gate Campground.

The trailhead for Mora Flats is at Iron Gate Campground. Follow the directions given for Hamilton Mesa, hike No. 4.

Begin hiking on the Hamilton Mesa Trail No. 249, immediately passing through a gate and entering the Pecos Wilderness. Begin a

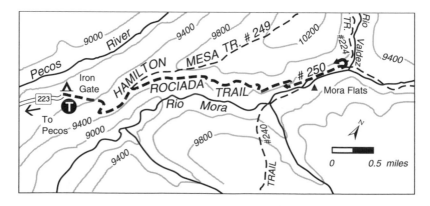

gentle climb through the fir forest to the top of a ridge. At the top, take a short spur trail to the right to an overlook into the deep Rio Mora Canyon. Here the main trail swings left (north) along the crest of the ridge, with several more viewpoints along the way.

After crossing a small aspen meadow 1 mile from the start, reach a junction and bear right onto Rociada Trail No. 250. The trail traverses a long, winding ridge high above the Rio Mora, passing through open stands of aspen along the way. In early summer, the ridge is covered with large yellow false pine lupines, wild iris, Richardson's geranium, wild strawberries, and more—as many as fifty wildflower species may be found in bloom. At mile 3.1, pass through a fence and enjoy a view of Mora Flats from above.

The trail now drops to Mora Flats through a series of switchbacks, reaching the meadow at mile 3.8. From the meadow edge, Trail No. 240 crosses the stream and leads to the main portion of the flats, while Trail No. 250 turns north to parallel the stream. Excellent campsites are found here and in another 0.5 mile near the junction with Rio Valdez. Return to the trailhead by the same route.

Rio Valdez in Mora Flats

6 LA BAJADA HILL

Managed by: Santa Fe National Forest, Española Ranger District
Distance: 4.5 miles, day hike
Elevation range: 5,500 to 6,100 feet
Elevation gain: 600 feet
Difficulty: easy
Seasons: mid-March to mid-May, September to December
Water: carry water
Map: USGS Tetilla Peak 7.5' quadrangle
Interesting features: El Camino Real, wagon ruts, historic road, petroglyphs

The decaying road up La Bajada Hill follows a segment of El Camino Real, the road used to connect New Spain (Mexico) and New Mexico from 1598. This stretch of the route, only a few miles from the end of the journey at Santa Fe, was one of the most difficult on the entire 600-mile trip from Chihuahua. Most of the time, travelers could follow the Santa Fe River through a deep canyon to reach the city. However, when high water prevented use of the easy route, travelers—often with ox-drawn wagons hauling a year's worth of supplies for colonists—were forced to climb a wall of ancient La Bajada Hill. It was difficult work going up; the trip down—braking wagons with ropes, rocks, and muscle power—was even more arduous.

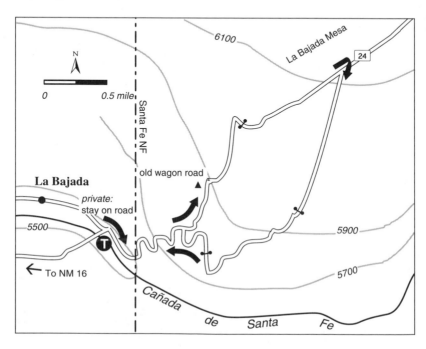

Historic petroglyphs inscribed by early automobile drivers on La Bajada Hill

A wagon road was scratched into the hillside by the United States Army in the 1860s, then improved to accommodate automobiles in the early 1900s. From the top of the hill, a less-steep road built in the 1920s offers an alternative return route. Little shade is found on the open slopes along the entire trip.

To reach the trailhead, take exit 264 off I 25 between Santa Fe and Albuquerque. Go west on NM 16 for 3.5 miles and turn right, following the signs for Tetilla Peak Recreation Area. In 1 mile, turn right on an unmarked gravel road that first parallels the paved one. After 1.5 miles, cross the Santa Fe River and park just past the bridge.

Looming over the trailhead is La Bajada Hill, a series of steplike terraces of basalt lava. Begin walking north and immediately turn right on a rocky gravel road that is the historic auto road up the hill. Stay on the road as it briefly traverses private land. Cross a small irrigation ditch and begin climbing on the first of several gentle switchbacks. As the road loops around basalt boulders, look for petroglyphs dating from the automobile era and older ones from the Pueblos.

After the switchbacks, come to a Y intersection about 0.75 mile from the start. The right fork is the return segment of this hike; bear left and follow the decomposing road surface across a long terrace of rock. In a few minutes, look to the left over the edge of the road. Just below is the wagon road built in the 1860s. Visually trace the route of the older road as it climbs the hillside below the newer route. After two hairpin turns, look right on a cliff face for more historic inscriptions on the rocks.

Pass through a gate and reach the top of the hill at mile 1.5. On the plains below, faint wagon ruts from El Camino Real are visible leading to the small village of La Bajada at the foot of the hill. Continue hiking north, now crossing the gently sloping flats leading to Santa Fe. At mile 2.2, turn right onto the first side road entering from the right. Walk downhill, angling to the southeast, toward Cañada de Santa Fe. Reach the edge of the canyon and enjoy the view down to the bottom. The road now swings south, passing through a gate and following the newest route down the hill. This section was blasted out of the basalt, and the walls are eroded back onto the roadway. At mile 3.1, enjoy another view to the plains below. Continue on the road, passing through another gate and dropping slowly to meet the route up the hill taken earlier. Backtrack down the steep switchbacks to return to the bridge.

7 CAJA DEL RIO CANYON

Managed by: Santa Fe National Forest, Española Ranger District
Distance: 6 miles, day hike
Elevation range: 5,450 to 5,850 feet
Elevation gain: 400 feet
Difficulty: easy
Seasons: September to May
Water: carry water
Map: USGS White Rock 7.5' quadrangle
Interesting features: spectacular small canyon through a volcano, scenic views, the Rio Grande

The trail-less route along Cañada Ancha through Caja del Rio Canyon leads through a small volcano. Locally, this canyon is called Diablo, and the devil had some fun here slicing a narrow cut through six-sided columns of hard basalt. The route follows a wash into the depths of White Rock Canyon and to the Rio Grande, reaching the river near the site of Buckman, a railhead for logging operations on the nearby mesas during the 1920s.

From Santa Fe, go north on US 84/285. In about 3 miles, turn left onto Camino de la Tierra. After 7.5 miles of winding through scattered

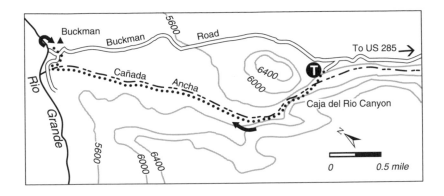

homes, the road turns to gravel. Continue on this road, which when dry is passable to all vehicles, to 15.5 miles from the highway. Bear left onto a track heading down to Cañada Ancha and park in the large open area near the wash.

Walk toward the slash in the rock wall by crossing a fence and walking down the bottom of Cañada Ancha. The wash soon enters the narrow canyon below soaring towers of brown basalt. To the right, the walls of the canyon are made of intricate patterns of cooled lava; the left side is a jumble of house-sized boulders that have crashed down from the cliffs above. Farther along, a streak of orange soil on the wall shows where flowing lava scorched the ground as it flowed over the surface about a million years ago. Hikers may be torn by conflicting desires to linger and enjoy this unique spot and to hustle to avoid being caught in a rockfall.

Toward the end of the narrows, a spring adds a trickle of water to the scene. Emerge from the narrow canyon to walk down a broad wash. To the right, views of the cliffs paint a detailed picture of the workings of a small volcano, with tilted and twisted layers of rock and a variety of colors and rock types. Continue downstream and enjoy the expanding view, which soon encompasses Otowi Peak, another small volcano straight ahead, and the airfall volcanic deposits of the Pajarito Plateau across the river. At about mile 1.7, the wash angles toward the northwest.

Cañada Ancha continues to widen. About 3 miles from the start, just before reaching the Rio Grande, intersect a dirt road that crosses the wash. Turn right onto the road and continue another 0.25 mile to intersect a road/arroyo combination in a thicket of tamarisk. Turn left and walk a few yards to the Rio Grande and the site of Buckman. Nothing remains of the bridge and buildings once found here, but across the river, Buckman Road can be seen winding up the orange cliffs.

To return, either backtrack up Cañada Ancha or, to avoid trudging up the sand, walk up Buckman Road to the trailhead.

8 SANTA BARBARA DIVIDE

Managed by: Carson National Forest, Pecos Wilderness, Camino Real
  Ranger District
Distance: 20 miles, one- or two-night backpack
Elevation range: 8,900 to 12,000 feet
Elevation gain: 3,500 feet
Difficulty: difficult
Seasons: late June to mid-October
Water: Rio Santa Barbara, West Fork
Maps: USGS Jicarita Peak and Pecos Falls 7.5' quadrangles, USFS Pecos
  Wilderness
Interesting features: pristine watershed, high mountain scenery, excellent
  fishing

Even in the arid mountains of the Southwest, logging has been common for the past one hundred years. Few watersheds have been as fortunate as that of the Rio Santa Barbara. The rugged slopes and remote location of its upper canyon have protected the forests from the ax and chainsaw. The Rio Santa Barbara watershed is the most pristine in New Mexico, remaining much the same as it was in the 1830s when American mountain men out of Taos, just a few miles to the north, trapped beaver in its waters. A walk along the clear, cold waters of the Santa Barbara is like traveling back in time.

The first 2 miles above the campground receive moderate use in summer, but the West Fork Trail beyond sees little traffic. Along the way, the view of the canyon of the West Fork and the humpbacked dome of 12,841-foot Chimayosos Peak is unforgettable. Among fishermen, the Santa Barbara has a reputation as one of the best places in the state to angle for cutthroat trout.

From Española, take NM 68 north 13.5 miles to NM 75 at Dixon. Turn left and continue to Peñasco, about 15 miles. About one mile past

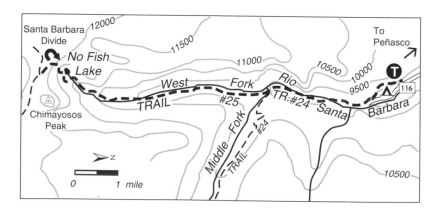

The humpbacked summit of Chimayosos Peak from the West Fork of the Rio Santa Barbara

the junction with NM 76, continue straight onto NM 73 as NM 75 turns sharply left. In another 1.5 miles, turn left onto FR 116 and follow the signs 4 miles to Santa Barbara Campground. Park at the trailhead near the campground entrance.

From the trailhead, begin hiking around the campground on Trail No. 24. Once past the last campsite, the trail swings close to the river. Soon high cliffs pinch the trail and stream together and, at mile 1.2, the trail enters the Pecos Wilderness. Cross a bridge over the river and begin a gentle climb along the east slope of the canyon. Continue above the river through old Douglas firs in the dense forest.

At a junction 2.2 miles from the start, bear right onto Trail No. 25, the West Fork Trail. Immediately reach a round meadow at the meeting of the Middle and West Forks of the Santa Barbara—a made-to-order rest or lunch spot. The trail continues to the other side of the meadow where it crosses the Middle Fork on a logjam. Use caution at the crossing and do not attempt it during spring runoff or other periods of high water.

From the crossing, the trail climbs slowly along the canyon of the West Fork in an open forest away from the stream. This is wild country, and a glimpse of deer, elk, or even a bear would not be unexpected. At mile 4, the trail bears right and emerges into a meadow high above the stream. The river below is puddled into large beaver ponds where brown trout can be seen sipping insects from the surface.

After another mile, the trail again enters the forest before crossing to the west side of the stream 6 miles from the start. Begin climbing the west wall of the canyon on a long series of gentle switchbacks. At mile 7.5, cross the West Fork again and pass several nice camping spots, the last ones before the divide. If backpacking, plan to camp here.

The trail now makes wild swings in its attempt to make the final assault on the ridge less difficult, but it is still a tough haul, lightened by stunning views of Chimayosos Peak to the east. Climb a rocky ridge and reach the divide where all the world is below. From the ridge, trails lead south into the Pecos watershed and east and west along the ridgeline. Enjoy the view, then return by the same route.

9 LA LUZ/TRAMWAY LOOP

Managed by: Cibola National Forest, Sandia Wilderness, Sandia Ranger District
Distance: 9 miles, day hike
Elevation range: 6,600 to 10,300 feet
Elevation gain: 3,900 feet
Difficulty: strenuous
Seasons: May to November
Water: at the tramway terminals, carry water
Maps: USGS Sandia Crest 7.5' quadrangle, USFS Sandia Wilderness
Interesting features: spectacular, rugged country; one-way hike

The combination of the La Luz Trail and the Sandia Peak Tramway offers hikers a unique opportunity for a challenging one-way hike. The Sandia Mountains are a round-shouldered hump of granite and limestone that dominates the eastern skyline of Albuquerque. The La Luz Trail climbs 3,600 feet from the base of the Sandias to the crest at 10,300 feet. From the summit, hikers can return via the same trail or opt to enjoy a relaxing 15-minute descent back to the base by riding the tram. As an alternative trip, hikers can take the tram to the top of the mountain and walk back to the base, a trip that is still quite demanding. One-way tram tickets for hikers can be purchased at either terminal. The tram generally runs between 9 a.m. and 5 p.m. Call (505) 298-8518 for the latest information.

The trailhead for the La Luz Trail is located at the Juan Tabo Picnic Area, but those interested in a loop hike need to begin at the Sandia Tramway parking area and take the Tramway Trail to connect with the La Luz Trail 1 mile above its bottom terminus. This is a popular trail, crowded on weekends with hikers, climbers, and trail runners. The trail has a long history of rerouting and there are many places where old trails may confuse inexperienced hikers. The current trail is well-worn its entire length. Note that the steep terrain limits the number of campsites along the trail.

From Albuquerque, take I 25 north to the Tramway Road exit, NM 556. Head east on NM 556 for 6 miles, then turn left to stay on Tramway

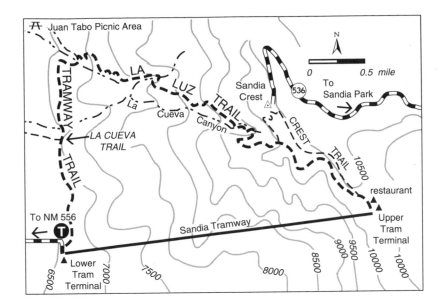

Road. One mile from the turn, enter the Sandia Peak Tramway grounds. After paying the nominal parking fee, park near the base of the tramway.

Begin hiking at the northeast corner of the parking lot at the information kiosk and sign for the Tramway Trail. Head into the granite boulder wonderland, immediately entering the Sandia Wilderness. The trail skirts along the foot of the mountains, passing near homes and private property, so stay on the trail. In 1 mile, pass the La Cueva Trail to the left and cross La Cueva Canyon. Climb a narrow ridge directly above some large homes, then cross the ridge and bear right, dropping into another canyon. Here the many switchbacks of the La Luz Trail are visible across the canyon. At mile 2.3, immediately after crossing the bottom of the canyon, intersect the La Luz Trail and turn right.

Begin the long journey through "Switchback City" where the trail builders arguably went overboard to ease the grades of the next 800-foot climb. The trail now skirts the north side of a deep canyon on a shadeless slope before reaching a tunnel of vegetation in the canyon bottom. Climb the south wall of the canyon to an open saddle, then continue the ascent on the north slope of La Cueva Canyon. Several broad switchbacks through oak scrub lead to a saddle over a small spur ridge. Drop from the saddle into the conifer forest of upper La Cueva Canyon.

Cross the bottom of La Cueva Canyon where a sign warns against further travel in winter. At this point the trail has gained 2,600 feet,

The La Luz Trail crosses a wide talus slope a dozen times.

with 1,300 feet to go. Take a deep breath and begin the steepest section of trail. The route is a long set of switchbacks that cross and recross a talus chute about a dozen times. Views of La Cueva Canyon and a huge granite slab to the right are impressive. One more set of broad meanders leads to a saddle and trail junction. The trail left goes to Sandia Crest; continue straight across the saddle on the La Luz Trail. Here the trail leaves the granite and travels along the base of a banded limestone cliff. This spectacular section of trail is perched on a wide ledge with nearby views of massive towers of granite. South Sandia Peak dominates the view in the distance.

At mile 8.9, reach the junction with the Crest Trail, which is usually crowded with tourists. To reach the upper tramway terminal, bear right across a wooden deck at a restaurant. The ticket window is in the USFS Visitor Center directly behind the tramway dock.

10 NORTH SANDIA CREST/ 10K LOOP

Managed by: Cibola National Forest, Sandia Ranger District
Distance: 7 miles, day hike
Elevation range: 9,800 to 10,600 feet
Elevation gain: 900 feet
Difficulty: moderate
Seasons: May to October
Water: Media Spring
Maps: USGS Sandia Crest 7.5' quadrangle
Interesting features: isolation on the edge of a major city, views

In contrast to the steep western face of the Sandia Mountains, the east side of the range gently slopes from the crest, creating less demanding terrain for hiking and cross-country skiing. The North Crest Trail offers views of both sides of the mountain, traveling along the ridge above vertical granite crags, with a short side trail leading to North Sandia Peak. The 10K Trail, so named because it roughly follows the 10,000-foot contour, drops through the sloping conifer forest of the east side of the range.

To reach the trailhead, go east from Albuquerque on I 40 to the Cedar Crest/Tijeras exit and follow the signs for NM 14 north. In 6 miles, turn left onto NM 536. Continue 14 miles to Sandia Crest and park in the large lot.

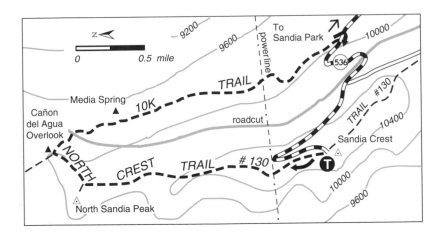

Begin by following the signs for the North Crest Trail No. 130. The trail skirts below a forest of radio and TV towers before entering the conifer woods and beginning to descend. Several short side trails lead to views to the west. Watch for Richardson's geraniums and larkspur under the firs and spruces and juncos and mountain chickadees in the trees. Continue through conifer forest along the rim, reaching an unmaintained side trail to North Sandia Peak at mile 1.7. This short trip leads to fantastic views of the granite spires and cliffs to the west. Back on the main trail, make a short descent and reach the Cañon del Agua Overlook at mile 2. Find the often unmarked 10K Trail at the edge of the clearing; watch for the blue diamonds that mark this as a ski trail. Turn right onto the 10K Trail and continue descending.

At mile 2.2, the trail crosses a broad road cut, a scar from a never-completed highway project. In a few minutes, pass a sign for Media Spring, which is misidentified as Osha Spring on some maps. Continue through the deep forest on a rolling trail, passing under a powerline at mile 3.8. Near NM 536, follow the main trail through a confusing stretch and reach the paved road near the road cut. Turn right and walk along the road just over 2 miles back to Sandia Crest.

Granite towers of the Sandia Mountains

11 | SOUTH SANDIA PEAK

Managed by: Cibola National Forest, Sandia Wilderness, Sandia Ranger District
Distance: 12 miles, day hike or backpack
Elevation range: 6,600 to 9,500 feet
Elevation gain: 2,300 feet
Difficulty: moderate
Seasons: May to October
Water: Cañoncito and South Sandia springs
Maps: USGS Sandia Crest and Tijeras 7.5' quadrangles, USFS Sandia
 Wilderness
Interesting features: isolation on the edge of a major city, views

Unlike the developed central section, the southern half of the Sandia
Mountains is isolated and wild, traversed by a half dozen interesting
trails. Hiking up the Cañoncito Trail and then walking the ridge to
South Sandia Peak leads through the heart of this country. Despite the
proximity of civilization, be on the watch for black bear, which are
common in the Sandias, and mountain lion tracks.

The hike requires setting up a short shuttle from the Canyon Estates
to the Cañoncito trailheads. Hikers looking for a loop trip can hike the
described route past South Sandia Spring to the Upper Faulty Trail
and can return to the Cañoncito Trailhead via the Upper or Lower
Faulty Trail. This variation is a 17-mile loop, which for most would be
a difficult day hike. Hikers attempting the loop should plan on an
overnight stay near South Sandia Peak, where water is available at
South Sandia Spring.

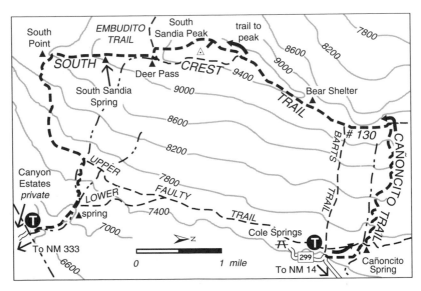

Set up the shuttle for this hike by driving east from Albuquerque on I 40. Five miles from the foot of Tijeras Pass, exit the highway at Tijeras/NM 337. At the foot of the exit ramp, turn left, immediately passing under the interstate. Bear right onto a dead-end road marked for Canyon Estates. Drive slowly through private land on Arrowhead Road about 0.5 mile to the parking area at the trailhead. Leave a vehicle, then backtrack under the interstate to NM 333. Turn left and in 0.1 mile, follow the signs for NM 14 and Cedar Crest, again bearing left under the interstate. Once on NM 14, continue 3.5 miles through Cedar Crest to FR 299, which is marked with a sign for Cole Springs Picnic Area and Cañoncito. Turn left, then in 0.4 mile, bear left again at a Y intersection. Take this rough dirt road 1.2 miles to the well-marked Cañoncito Trailhead. The last 0.5 mile of this route often requires a high-clearance vehicle.

From the trailhead, climb steeply to the right on the Cañoncito Trail, avoiding the more prominent Barts Trail straight ahead. The trail soon bears left to head up canyon, reaching streamside near some interesting travertine terraces. After crossing the stream, watch for a sign pointing to Cañoncito Spring. Just beyond, come to a four-way intersection with the Faulty Trail. Continue straight on the Cañoncito Trail, immediately entering the Sandia Wilderness. The trail begins to climb steeply on limestone rocks, many of which are adorned with fossilized sea life.

As the trail climbs, it traverses a dry, oak-scrub woodland with abundant agave and prickly pear. At mile 1.5, climb on broad switchbacks before the ascent steepens all the way to the South Crest Trail No. 130, reached at mile 3.2. Turn left onto the South Crest Trail and stop for a break in 200 feet at an overlook of Albuquerque and the Sandia Tramway.

Continue south on the Crest Trail, passing the Barts Trail to the left at mile 3.7. Fine views to the west are found along the route. Pass Bear Shelter at mile 4.3. The trail travels through aspen groves, oak stands, and meadows as it heads toward South Sandia Peak, which is first visible at mile 5.2. Climb the peak by leaving the South Crest Trail at a small saddle and following the ridgeline. (The main trail stays on the south flank of the peak, skirting the base to Deer Pass, 6.7 miles from the start.) Eventually pick up a faint trail on the west (right) side of the ridgeline. This trail becomes more distinct near the base of the peak, where a side trail to the left climbs straight up to the summit.

From the top, backtrack down the steep side trail to the path on the west side of South Sandia Peak. Turn left and stay on the trail near the ridgeline, now heading south. After walking this trail for 0.7 mile, cross a saddle and intersect the Embudito Trail. Bear left, descending to rejoin the South Crest Trail at Deer Pass.

Turn right onto the South Crest Trail, descending into a drainage. Pass South Sandia Spring at mile 6.9, then begin the broad switchbacks that lead down from the crest. At mile 8.5, pass South Point, the last of the viewpoints on the ridge. For the next 2 miles, descend steeply through drainages and over spur ridges. At mile 10.5, the upper Faulty Trail angles off to the left. Continue straight on the South Sandia Trail, winding down many switchbacks on a ridge above

Hiker overlooking limestone beds of Sandia Crest (June Fabryka-Martin photo)

two dry drainages. At mile 11.2, intersect the lower Faulty Trail to the left and continue straight. Soon pass a small spring, then bear right at a Y intersection. After passing a cave, continue to descend to the Canyon Estates Trailhead.

49

NORTHERN SANGRE DE CRISTO MOUNTAINS

Descending into the Rio Grande Gorge on the Cebolla Mesa Trail
(Jessica Martin photo)

12   LOBO PEAK

Managed by: Carson National Forest, Columbine-Hondo Wilderness Study Area, Questa Ranger District
Distance: 11 miles, day hike or backpack
Elevation range: 8,400 to 12,100 feet
Elevation gain: 3,800 feet
Difficulty: strenuous
Seasons: late June to October
Water: Manzanita Creek, Italianos Creek
Maps: USGS Arroyo Seco and Wheeler Peak 7.5' quadrangles
Interesting features: challenging climb; cool, shady trail; unique views

At 12,115 feet, Lobo Peak is the highest point in the small range of mountains that lie between the Rio Hondo and the Red River. The mountains rise abruptly from the bordering canyons, forcing the trail to Lobo Peak to gain almost 4,000 feet in 4.5 miles. Lobo Peak's isolation from other high points makes the views from the top unique, taking in the Taos Plateau and Rio Grande Gorge to the west, the Latir Peaks to the north, and the Wheeler Peak area to the south.

From Taos, go north and west on US 64 for 3 miles to the junction with NM 150. Turn right, following the signs for the Taos Ski Area. Continue about 12 miles from US 64 (2 miles from Upper Cuchilla Campground) and park at the trailhead for the Manzanita Trail.

The first section of the Manzanita Trail is on private land. Begin on a dirt road, passing through a gate, then bearing left to parallel Manzanita Creek and entering Carson National Forest. At mile 0.8, where water from a spring drains along the route, the road becomes a true

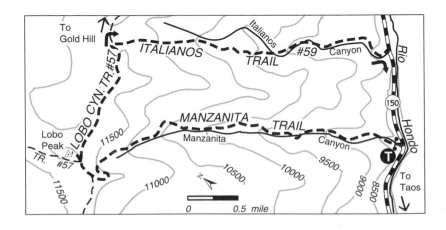

trail. In a few minutes, make the first of many crossings of Manzanita Creek over the next 0.5 mile.

At mile 1.5, climb two switchbacks and parallel the stream higher on the slope. For the next mile, the grade steepens as the trail becomes almost like a staircase in places. At mile 2.6, the trail bends left to cross a dry drainage, then resumes the steep climb. Cross the base of a small talus slope, then enter a clearing offering views of the ridge to the east. Another clearing is reached at mile 3.7, this one offering views of the high ridgeline to the north. At an unmarked intersection, bear left, then begin walking a series of switchbacks to the top of a narrow ridge. Turn right with the ridgeline and enter a small meadow with great views in all directions. Continue along the ridge, watching carefully for the trail when it crosses open areas. At the junction with Lobo Canyon Trail No. 57, at mile 4.5, go straight to reach the summit of Lobo Peak.

After enjoying the view from the summit, return to the junction of the Lobo Peak and Manzanita trails. Turn left (northeast) onto the Lobo Canyon Trail, following a ridgeline in the direction of Gold Hill. At mile 5.5, skirt the base of a rocky crag before the trail becomes faint as it passes to the left of a small peak. The trail then drops steeply to a saddle.

At the saddle, turn right onto the Italianos Canyon Trail No. 59. Several quick switchbacks lead to a nice campsite near a small spring. Look carefully for the trail as it leaves the marshy area and climbs the toe of a small ridge. At mile 6.6, reach a meadow where the trail disappears, but a rock cairn visible on the other side of the clearing marks the route. Continue to drop through small meadows and open conifer forest, passing plenty of fine campsites along the way. After a brief flat stretch, descend through switchbacks at mile 8.1 to cross the main stream in Italianos Canyon. The trail remains wet for the next mile, crossing the stream many times. More campsites are found between mile 9 and 10. At mile 10, exit the canyon and reach NM 150. Turn right and walk 1 mile to the Manzanita Trailhead.

Pikas are common on talus in the Sangre de Cristos.

13   WHEELER PEAK

Managed by: Carson National Forest, Wheeler Peak Wilderness, Questa
Ranger District
Distance: 14 miles, day hike or backpack
Elevation range: 9,400 to 13,161 feet
Elevation gain: 3,700 feet
Difficulty: strenuous
Seasons: late June to October
Water: Middle Fork of the Red River
Maps: USGS Wheeler Peak 7.5' quadrangle, USFS Latir and Wheeler Peak
Wilderness
Interesting features: long walk above tree line, spectacular views

As the highest point in New Mexico, 13,161-foot Wheeler Peak is a
popular destination for hikers. Although for the first several miles the
route is confusing, a well-worn trail with moderate grades leads to the
summit, passing through the state's most extensive area of alpine vegetation. Eye-popping views extend in all directions from the long ridge
leading to the peak; a small herd of bighorn sheep and the rare chance
to see white-tailed ptarmigan add to the attraction.

A safe hike to Wheeler Peak requires a good deal of common sense.
High elevation makes sunscreen mandatory on this trip, even on
cloudy days. Snow remains on the upper trail into early or even late
July when the summer thunderstorm season makes it dangerous to be
on the ridge. Start early to get off the peak by noon. September is the
best time to make the climb, but hikers should know the weather
forecast before starting the trip: intensive snowstorms can hit the
mountains any time after late August. The trip to Wheeler Peak is a

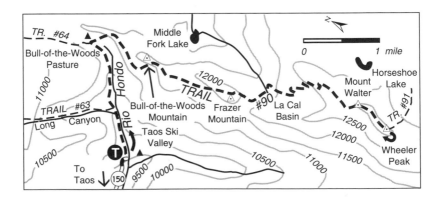

long one and hikers should allow 10 to 12 hours for the round trip to the summit.

From Taos, go north and west on US 64 for 3 miles to the junction with NM 150. Turn right, following the signs for the Taos Ski Area. Continue about 15 miles and park in the upper gravel lot at Taos Ski Valley near an information board.

From the trailhead, follow the signs and begin hiking northeast along the headwaters of the Rio Hondo. For the first 3 miles, the route is part road and part trail, and it passes many confusing side trails and roads. The route is poorly marked; when in doubt, hikers should follow the most heavily used trail. The route begins near the canyon bottom, then climbs briefly before intersecting the Long Canyon Trail No. 63 at mile 0.9. Shortly after this junction, the route follows an old road along the north slope of the canyon, with views back to Taos Ski Area. At mile 1.9, reach Bull-of-the-Woods Pasture and the intersection with the Gold Hill Trail No. 64. Follow the road to the right, skirting the west side of Bull-of-the-

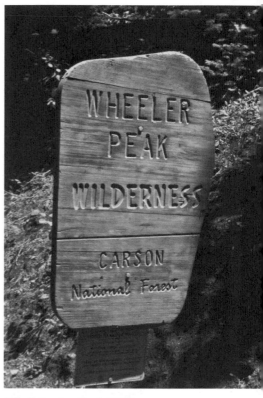

The Wheeler Peak Wilderness protects New Mexico's most extensive area of alpine terrain.

Woods Mountain. The road climbs to the ridgeline and, at mile 2.9, meets an easy-to-follow trail that parallels the ridge.

The trail, now above tree line, continues along the ridge, passing the summit of Frazer Mountain at mile 4.1. Descend into the headwaters of the Middle Fork of the Red River, which offers limited campsites and water at mile 5. The trail resumes the climb, passing the La Cal Basin. Another steep mile in thin air leads to the ridgeline. At mile 6.8, reach the summit of Mount Walter. Descend briefly to a saddle, then climb the final 0.25 mile to the summit of Wheeler Peak.

While keeping an eye on the weather, enjoy the view, which takes in the highest peaks of the Sangre de Cristos as well as parts of the Rio Grande Gorge. Return to the trailhead by the same route.

14 SOUTH BOUNDARY TRAIL

Managed by: Carson National Forest, Camino Real Ranger District
Distance: 13 miles one-way, day hike or backpack
Elevation range: 7,300 to 10,300 feet
Elevation gain: 300 feet; 3,300 foot descent
Difficulty: moderate
Seasons: late May to late October
Water: American Spring
Maps: USGS Shady Brook and Ranchos de Taos 7.5' quadrangles
Interesting features: historic trail, views of Wheeler Peak Wilderness, quiet
   solitude

The South Boundary Trail—so named because it runs parallel to the
dividing line between the former Taos and Rio Grande del Rancho land
grants—travels the length of the Fernando Mountains. The trail was
blazed in the early 1800s by ranchers as a route to drive sheep from
Taos to grazing areas in the high country. Traversing the north side of
the ridge, the route is a long, shady walk through deep Douglas-fir and
spruce forest. The first 10 miles of the hike descend gently; the last 3
miles are very steep.

To do this hike as a one-way descent, set up a shuttle by leaving a
vehicle at the El Nogal Picnic Area 3 miles out of Taos on US 64. Continue east on US 64 for 10 miles beyond the picnic area and turn right
onto FR 437. In 0.4 mile, stay on FR 437 by turning right, heading for
Garcia Park. Continue 6 miles to the junction with FR 445 to the right
and park.

From FR 437, walk west on the wide dirt FR 445 through open
stands of aspen, spruce, and fir. At 0.7 mile, come to a four-way intersection. Trail No. 164 enters from the left and continues into the woods
to the right, but it is difficult to follow in this stretch. Turn right to
stay on FR 445.

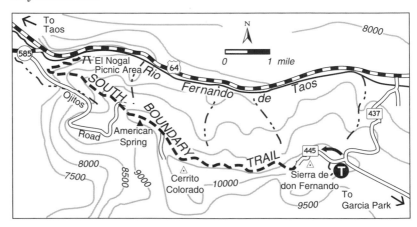

At mile 1, pass a road to the left and begin a gentle climb to skirt around Sierra de don Fernando, passing great views of the Wheeler Peak Wilderness to the right. At mile 1.5, begin descending around the northwest base of Sierra de don Fernando. At the bottom of the descent at mile 2.1, leave the road by walking over a berm to the left and picking up a trail heading south. Angle into a small meadow where the trail becomes faint. Look for rock cairns and trail markers in the tall grass. After descending from the top of a small knoll, the trail bears right at a large cairn and is now easier to follow.

Descending through a closed forest, the trail joins an abandoned road. At mile 3.1, bear left. From here the route is often marked with large rock cairns. At a fence in a few hundred yards, bear right off the old road and onto a trail. Begin a long, wonderful, ever-so-gently descending stroll through thick conifer forest, stands of aspen, and oak scrub.

Elk tooth marks on aspens

At mile 6.2, enter a large meadow at the base of Cerrito Colorado, where several scenic campsites are found. At mile 7.2, the trail crosses to the south side of the ridge. Just beyond a small saddle, intersect a road angling back sharply to the left. Bear right as the trail follows the road, passing through drier oak-scrub woodland, then cross to the north side of the ridgeline. At mile 8.5, walk through a four-way intersection and continue straight on the main trail. Soon pass American (Bear) Spring. Beyond the spring, bear right as a trail enters from the left and continue straight as the trail joins an abandoned road.

At mile 9.3, a sign indicates the trail goes right, but continue straight ahead on the road. In 0.2 mile, meet the Ojitos Road at a four-way intersection and continue straight. From this point, the trail descends steeply on a rocky surface through open woods. At mile 10.5, reach a small saddle on the ridgeline. The trail drops to the south side of the ridge and becomes very steep. When the trail again meets the top of the ridge, turn left at a T intersection. At a Y intersection, bear right off the northwest side of the ridge. At mile 12.2, the trail angles sharply back to the south. Take a sharp switchback to the right, avoiding another branch of the trail straight ahead. Turn through several broad switchbacks descending the north flank of the ridge. At mile 13, reach another trail junction, continue straight, and then make a sharp left. Cross the bridge over the Rio Fernando de Taos and enter the El Nogal Picnic Area.

15 BARRANCA HILL

Managed by: Carson National Forest, Tres Piedras Ranger District, Bureau of Land Management, Taos Resource Area
Distance: 9 miles, day hike
Elevation range: 6,200 to 6,950 feet
Elevation gain: 800 feet
Difficulty: moderate
Seasons: late March to early May, September to late October
Water: carry water
Maps: USGS Carson, Taos Junction, and Velarde 7.5' quadrangles
Interesting features: historic railroad grade, railroad artifacts, remote canyon scenery

When the Denver and Rio Grande Railroad engineers went looking for a location to drop 1,000 feet from the Taos Plateau to the bottom of the Rio Grande Gorge, they found a suitable place in Comanche Canyon. After the construction of a small station at the top of the grade named Barranca (ravine), the steep grade below acquired the name Barranca Hill. It was the most infamous stretch on the railroad, requiring special braking procedures on the descent and a double head—two engines—for the climb up.

The railroad folded in 1942. Fifty years of erosion have covered much of the grade in rubble, and short detours are now necessary to get past ravines once spanned by small bridges. Along the way are an abundance of artifacts: rock inscriptions, wooden culverts, old trestle timbers, rail spikes, and more. Hikers should remember to leave all artifacts where they are found.

To reach the trailhead, take US 84/285 from Española through Ojo Caliente and past the junction with NM 111, which is about 25 miles from Española. Nine miles beyond NM 111, at Taos Junction, turn right onto NM 567 and immediately turn right again onto FR 557. This rutted dirt road requires a high-clearance vehicle. Drive on FR 557 for 8 miles, parking at the junction with FR 557G and FR 557F.

Hike down the raised gravel FR 557G, which is directly on top of the railroad grade. At mile 0.8, come to a corral and stock pond. The grade angles through the corral and into the sharp cut in the basalt flows to

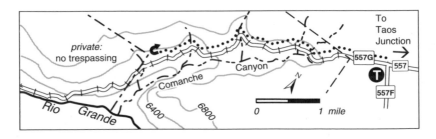

the southwest. Climb the fence on the west side of the corral and walk the corral fence to a gap. Turn right past a large juniper tree and angle toward the cut in the rocks ahead where gravel and rotting railroad ties are strewn along the route. Enter the cut and marvel that a railroad once passed this way.

Through the cut, the gravel railbed becomes easier to follow. The route is now in the very head of Comanche Canyon. Walk down canyon, soon coming to a rockfall blocking the grade. Follow a path to the left. For the next 0.25 mile, walk downhill on the grade through sagebrush, crossing a number of original wooden culverts along the way. The grade swings right through a short cut, then comes to the first major missing trestle. Leave the grade and follow the path to the right. Before climbing up the other side, notice the huge timbers still in place below the grade.

A few hundred feet beyond, another gap in the grade is the site of the second missing trestle. Skirt this obstacle by descending on the rocks to the left and climbing the other side. Once on the grade again, hikers are forced to pick a route through a long rockfall that blocks the grade. From here, the obstacles are easier to pass. Continue downhill

Trains once passed through this narrow cut on Barranca Hill.

on the west wall of Comanche Canyon, enjoying the widening view. Several small missing trestles are easily skirted on well-worn pathways. At mile 3.1, a long detour right takes you around another gap in the grade. Although other small rockfalls stand in the way, the route now is an easy stroll.

Just over 4 miles from the start, the grade reaches a steep arroyo with another missing bridge. This makes a good turnaround point. Note that 0.25 mile beyond the arroyo, the railroad grade enters private land. Do not cross the fence at the boundary. Retrace your steps back up the hill, enjoying the gentle slope carefully designed by the railroad engineers.

16   CEBOLLA MESA/ BIG ARSENIC TRAILS

Managed by: Carson National Forest, Questa Ranger District, Bureau of
    Land Management, Rio Grande Wild and Scenic River, Taos Resource Area
Distance: 8 miles, day hike or backpack
Elevation range: 6,600 to 7,360 feet
Elevation gain: 1,300 feet
Difficulty: moderate
Seasons: March to November
Water: Red River, Little and Big Arsenic Springs
Map: USGS Guadalupe Mountain 7.5' quadrangle
Interesting features: deep, rugged canyon; large river; fishing

As the Rio Grande flows over the thick sheets of lava that emanated from the volcanoes of the Taos Plateau, it has carved a gorge 60 miles long and up to 1,000 feet deep. The river within remains wild and free-flowing, fed by snowmelt in Colorado's San Juan Mountains and by thousands of springs within the gorge itself. The basalt walls are steep and house-sized boulders have tumbled from the walls to line the river or break the current as in-stream rocks. The polished rocks at

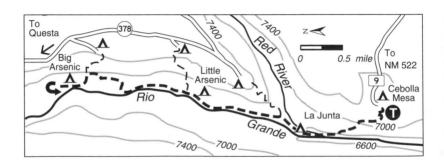

The Rio Grande from the Cebolla Mesa Trail

streamside are slick, and the water off the banks is often 10 feet deep. Ducks, mergansers, geese, and bald eagles are frequently seen from along the river.

Several trails enter the gorge from the Bureau of Land Management's Rio Grande Wild and Scenic River Recreation Area north and west of Questa, but entering the gorge via Cebolla Mesa requires less driving from Taos. The well-maintained Cebolla Mesa Trail leads to the confluence of the Red River and the Rio Grande and some of the best fishing in the state. Plenty of campsites are available within the gorge; particularly attractive are the shelters and firepits at La Junta, Little Arsenic, and Big Arsenic primitive campgrounds.

To reach the trailhead from Taos, head north on US 64 about 4 miles to the junction with NM 522. Continue straight on NM 522 for about 16 miles to FR 9. Turn left onto this rutted dirt road, which is passable to all vehicles when dry. Drive the length of FR 9, bearing left at an intersection 1 mile from the highway, and arrive at the Cebolla Mesa Campground in 3.5 miles.

The Cebolla Mesa Trail quickly drops from the rim on a series of steep switchbacks, passing through mixed vegetation that includes everything from yuccas to Douglas firs. Views of the river and the gorge are spectacular on the entire 1-mile descent. At the Rio Grande, a footbridge crosses the Red River into La Junta Campground. Follow the trail as it winds through the shelters and climbs a low ridge that separates the two rivers.

Heading north, the trail stays on the low divide, offering views up the canyon of the Red River. In 0.25 mile from the bridge, the La Junta Trail branches right to climb to the rim. Bear left and immediately drop to the Rio Grande. Continue up canyon, at times climbing to the bench above the river to avoid large rock falls. Pass the Little Arsenic shelters, the Little Arsenic Trail leading to the rim, and 0.25 mile beyond the shelters, the spring just to the right of the trail.

At mile 3.5, the trail ascends steeply to avoid a massive rockfall that stretches to the river. From the bench above the river, the climb continues over a low mound of boulders. Just beyond, meet the trail descending from Big Arsenic Campground on the rim. Before the next descent back to river level, more shelters are visible on the flat below. Again along the river, enjoy the shade of the trees and shelters at Big Arsenic. The springs are on the opposite side of the flat. Return to the trailhead by the same route.

17 HEART LAKE

Managed by: Carson National Forest, Latir Wilderness, Questa Ranger District
Distance: 11 miles, day hike or backpack
Elevation range: 9,200 to 12,100 feet
Elevation gain: 3,000 feet
Difficulty: strenuous
Seasons: mid-June to late September
Water: Lake Fork, Bull Creek, and Heart Lake
Maps: USGS Red River and Latir Peak 7.5' quadrangles
Interesting features: grand views above tree line, alpine lake, running water

At the close of the most recent Ice Age, glaciers melted from the highest peaks of the Sangre de Cristo Range and left behind a dozen small lakes in cirques at the heads of the valleys. Located in the Latir Wilderness, Heart Lake is only 5 miles from the trailhead. It is an easy climb from the lake to the alpine ridgeline above, where grand views reach from the Latir Lakes into Colorado. This trip is well worth an overnight stay, although camping is not permitted within 300 feet of Heart Lake or in the meadow surrounding Baldy Cabin. The shallow lake provides marginal habitat for trout, but Lake Fork holds a healthy population of pan-sized brook trout.

To get to the trailhead at Cabresto Lake from the intersection of NM 522 and NM 38 in Questa, turn onto NM 38 for 0.25 mile. Turn left onto NM 563 and travel 2.1 miles, then turn right onto gravel FR 134. Cross into Carson National Forest and drive 3.3 miles to FR 134A. Turn left and continue 2.1 miles to Cabresto Lake and campground. This road is

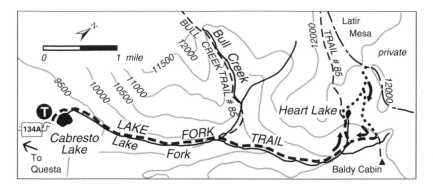

rough in places, so a high-clearance vehicle is recommended, although carefully driven sedans can make the trip.

The Lake Fork Trail starts by skirting to the left (west) of Cabresto Lake, then makes a long, steady climb parallel to Lake Fork of Cabresto Creek. The first 2 miles traverse conifer forest with cork-bark fir dominating the slopes. After passing through several small meadows, meet the Bull Creek Trail No. 85 about 2.5 miles from the start. Bear right, cross Bull Creek, and continue along Lake Fork.

After climbing the only switchback on the trail, enter a blue spruce forest. At mile 3.5, find a long meadow with excellent campsites on both sides of Lake Fork. In 0.5 mile, the trail re-enters the forest and climbs a low ridge. At mile 4.5, bear left toward Heart Lake at the junction with the Baldy Mountain Trail. In a few minutes, enter a small meadow and bear right to parallel small streams on both the left and right. As the trail peters out, again pick up the main trail to the left of the streams. From here it is a short distance to Heart Lake.

To reach the saddle above the lake, stay on the left side of the lake, passing the junction with Trail No. 85 on the left. Pick up the drainage to the north, following the drainage through a meadow. In the trees on the other side of the meadow, a trail switchbacks up to the saddle. Climb along the ridgeline to get excellent views of Heart and the Latir lakes as well as the mountains to the north. Do not cross onto private land on the north side of the ridge.

Return to the meadow below the saddle, but stay left on a route that cuts across a low ridge at the base of a talus slope. After crossing a low saddle, pick up a trail heading across a meadow, with a full view of Baldy Mountain straight ahead. Continue about 0.5 mile to a major intersection. Bear left toward Baldy Mountain to reach Baldy Cabin and a superb high meadow; turn right to return to Cabresto Lake. In the meadow's short grass, the trail tread to the right is not visible for the first 300 feet, but it is well-worn after that. Continue downhill to a sharp right turn across a dry drainage; immediately on the opposite side is the signed trail intersection where this trip previously had turned west to Heart Lake. This time, go straight to backtrack downhill to Cabresto Lake.

18   HORSESHOE LAKE

Managed by: Carson National Forest, Wheeler Peak Wilderness, Questa
Ranger District
Distance: 13.5 miles, backpack
Elevation range: 9,400 to 11,950 feet
Elevation gain: 2,800 feet
Difficulty: strenuous
Seasons: late June to mid-October
Water: forks of the Red River, Horseshoe and Lost lakes
Map: USGS Wheeler Peak 7.5' quadrangle
Interesting features: alpine scenery, high lakes, fishing, wildlife

Horseshoe and Lost lakes lie in rugged bowls at the foot of the highest ridge in New Mexico. The trail to the lakes is surprisingly gentle,
threading through deep conifer forest up and above the canyon of the
East Fork of the Red River. Ample campsites are available along the
way, and this beautiful area invites more than a day trip. Both lakes
host good populations of trout and are popular destinations for fishermen. From Horseshoe Lake it is a short trip to the summit of Wheeler
Peak, but extending the hike in this manner should be attempted only
as part of an overnight trip. Hikers can eliminate the road portion of
this hike with a short 2-mile shuttle by leaving a car or a mountain
bike at the Middle Fork Lake trailhead, then driving to start the hike
at the East Fork Trailhead.

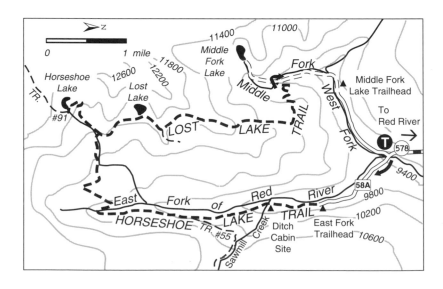

Horseshoe Lake is backed by the highest ridge in New Mexico.
(June Fabryka-Martin photo)

From the east end of the town of Red River, take NM 578 south for 6.4 miles to the end of the pavement and park. Begin walking on FR 58A to the east of the parking area and immediately cross the East Fork of the Red River. Bear right and follow the road through the small summer home development 1 mile to the East Fork Trailhead. Pick up the Horseshoe Lake Trail over a large dirt berm to the left, parallel to the East Fork to the right. Continue up this abandoned road to Ditch Cabin Site, cross Sawmill Creek on a bridge, and finally begin hiking on a trail at mile 1.7. The trail begins a gentle ascent through mixed conifer forest, which is rich in wildflowers—calypso orchids, false Solomon's Seal, Colorado columbine, monkshood, and cow parsnip—all summer long.

At mile 2.5, pass the intersection with the Sawmill Park Trail No. 55 to the left and continue up the canyon of the East Fork. At mile 3.9, drop down to cross the East Fork on a bridge. The trail now climbs several broad switchbacks, wandering through forest, meadow, and talus, with Red Cone often visible on the ridge to the left. As the trail crosses a small ridge, the high ridgeline that includes Wheeler Peak and Mount Walter stretches out in front. After crossing a bridge, reach a trail junction. Turn left to begin the climb to Horseshoe Lake, which is reached 0.7 mile from the junction. Camping is not permitted within 300 feet of the lake.

Backtrack down from Horseshoe Lake to the main trail. At the junction, turn left, heading toward Lost Lake. The trail loses elevation and crosses two wide talus slopes. A mile from the trail junction, reach Lost Lake. Many fine campsites are located away from the lake, which holds plenty of cutthroat and rainbow trout.

Continuing down from the lake, pass an old trail to the right, then leave the Wheeler Peak Wilderness. The trail now offers superb views to the north and east as it heads north through forest and talus. At mile 9.2, the trail begins to switchback down from the ridge and enters a deep conifer forest. Over the next 2 miles, the trail drops 1,500 feet to the intersection with Middle Fork Lake Road. Bear right and walk down the narrow road, which continues to switchback down the slope. At mile 12, cross a bridge over the West Fork of the Red River. Turn right onto the road parallel to the Middle Fork, soon passing the Middle Fork Lake Trailhead. Continue on the road just over a mile to reach the parking area.

19 SAWMILL PARK

Managed by: Carson National Forest, Wheeler Peak Wilderness, Questa Ranger District
Distance: 11 miles, day hike or backpack
Elevation range: 9,600 to 11,000 feet
Elevation gain: 1,500 feet
Difficulty: easy
Seasons: late May to late October
Water: Sawmill Creek
Maps: USGS Wheeler Peak and Eagle Nest 7.5' quadrangles
Interesting features: easy hike into a long, high meadow

The 3-mile-long meadow by Sawmill Creek is one of New Mexico's easiest-to-reach high country destinations. The grades of this trail are gentle enough for beginning backpackers. Idyllic campsites are found

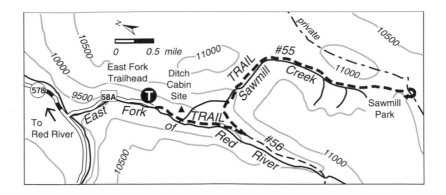

at the west end of the meadow and in the basins of several side drainages that enter from the west. Most visitors to the Wheeler Peak Wilderness head for the rim country to the west; it is likely that hikers will have Sawmill Park to themselves.

From the east end of the town of Red River, take NM 578 south for 6.4 miles to the end of the pavement. Bear left, cross a bridge, and take the gravel FR 58A, the right fork. Continue through private land on the rough road. After about 1 mile, pass through two gates, then bear left at a fork. Park at the East Fork Trailhead 1.4 miles from the pavement.

Begin hiking on a bermed four-wheel drive road angling uphill into the trees. Climb steadily for 0.4 mile to reach a small meadow, the site of Ditch Cabin. Cross Sawmill Creek on a small bridge, then begin a long, well-graded climb parallel to the East Fork of the Red River.

At a well-marked intersection 1.5 miles from the start, turn left onto the Sawmill Park Trail No. 55. This trail continues the easy climb up the east wall of the East Fork Canyon, crossing into the Wheeler Peak Wilderness. Once over the ridge, the trail again meets Sawmill Creek and follows the creek upstream and enters Sawmill Meadow. Pick up the tread of the trail near the trees at the north edge of the meadow. From here, the trail follows the meadow, bursting with wildflowers all summer long, with small but deep Sawmill Creek meandering through the tall grass. Stay on the trail to prevent damage to the meadow. Watch for deer, elk, and snowshoe hare in the forest openings.

About 3 miles from the start, the meadow and trail swing south. The valley narrows and widens several times before reaching Sawmill Park 4.9 miles from the start. The trail is easy to follow to a lone Douglas-fir tree standing at the meadow's edge. From the tree, follow the meadow south as it slopes up to a saddle. Here the meadow is always wet and alive with white marsh marigolds. At the saddle, a fence marks the boundary of private property. Return to the trailhead by the same route.

Wild irises above the grassy Sawmill Meadow

20   COMANCHE CREEK

Managed by: Carson National Forest, Valle Vidal Unit, Questa Ranger District
Distance: 6 miles, day hike
Elevation range: 9,250 to 9,650 feet
Elevation gain: 500 feet
Difficulty: easy
Seasons: late May to late October
Water: Comanche Creek
Map: USGS Comanche Point 7.5' quadrangle
Interesting features: rocky-sided valley, mountain vistas, fishing, historic trail

The valley of Comanche Creek is quintessential Valle Vidal. The open and expansive grasslands surrounding the creek are characteristic of the area, giving hikers a feeling of unconfined freedom and joy. This route follows Comanche Creek 2 miles before climbing to grand views from the mesas above. Near the site of La Belle, a once-thriving gold-mining community near the head of La Belle Creek, the route turns back through a narrows to Comanche Creek. Rumor has it this is the same route taken by Tom Ketchum, one of the last train robbers, when he rode from his hangout in Valle Vidal to Saturday night dances in La Belle, his identity unknown to the local townsfolk.

To reach the trailhead, take NM 522 north of Taos 40 miles to NM 196 at Costilla. Turn right on this paved then all-weather gravel road. Seventeen miles from NM 522, at the Carson National Forest boundary, the road becomes FR 1950. Six-and-a-half miles beyond the forest boundary, bear right on an unmarked dirt track heading from FR 1950 down toward Comanche Creek. Park at the wide turnout before the gate about 0.5 mile from FR 1950.

From the parking area, continue along the old road that parallels Comanche Creek, immediately passing through a gate. At mile 0.5, at the mouth of La Belle Creek, the return leg of this hike, walk beneath some dramatic outcrops of granite before crossing the stream and climbing to another gate. Two more stream crossings lead to Clayton Camp and a large ranch building to the left. A branch of the road leads to the sometimes active cattle camp, so stay to the right, passing the junction with Vidal Creek at mile 1.8.

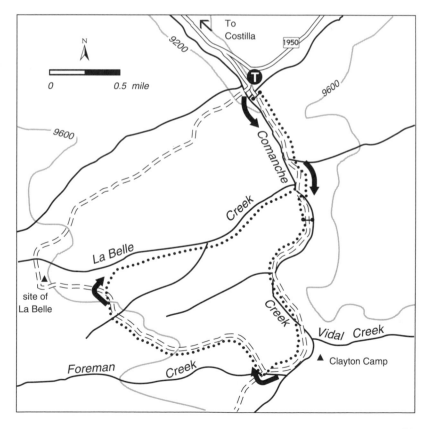

Beyond Clayton Camp, the road rounds a knoll on the right side of Comanche Creek before heading up Foreman Creek at mile 2.3. At a faint junction, the main trail up Comanche Creek bears left across a boggy area; bear slightly right onto a faint road that turns up a small grassy drainage heading northwest. The route follows the traces of the road. Climb to a low ridge, passing a small ruin to the left. On the ridge, the faint road turns left to follow the crest. Look back to the east for a glimpse of a huge, grassy bowl. This valley is Valle Vidal, from which the entire area takes its name.

About 3 miles from the start, the road bears slightly to the right, now heading northwest. Descend through a drainage and climb to another ridge. Once to the other side, look to the head of the valley to the site of La Belle, a once-thriving gold camp from the 1890s. Leave the old road, and drop into the broad valley of La Belle Creek to the right. Near the bottom of the valley, turn right and follow the stream down to Comanche Creek, which is about 1.5 miles away. Cross Comanche Creek and pick up the old road, turning left to return about 0.5 mile to the trailhead.

Open grassland valleys are characteristic of Valle Vidal.

21   McCRYSTAL PLACE

Managed by: Carson National Forest, Valle Vidal Unit, Questa Ranger District
Distance: 7 miles, day hike
Elevation range: 8,100 to 8,700 feet
Elevation gain: 700 feet
Difficulty: easy
Seasons: late May to late October
Water: McCrystal Creek
Maps: USGS Van Bremmer Park and Ash Mountain 7.5' quadrangles
Interesting features: impressive homestead ruins

In the late nineteenth century, the sprawling Maxwell Land Grant covered over a million acres of the northern Sangre de Cristo Mountains. That such a huge piece of prime real estate was not in the public domain was too much for some neighbors to accept. Many small ranchers established homesteads on the grant, believing that eventually the land would be rightfully declared open to the public. The grant managers called them squatters.

John McCrystal moved his family to a small valley watered by a small stream draining off Costilla Peak. Despite the knowledge that the land belonged to the Maxwell Grant, he boldly built his house and ranch and soon became a leader among the anti-grant men. As the courts upheld the rights of the grant, pressure on the ranchers increased. In 1890 he was forced to settle with the grant and purchased 320 acres for $960.

The old road to the McCrystal Place travels 3 miles along McCrystal Creek, offering a solid view of homesteading around the turn of the century. Even in ruins, one can see why the ranch was worth fighting for. Cattle still graze the rich meadows along McCrystal Creek; timber is plentiful in the surrounding hills. The peaceful view from McCrystal's yard extends many miles to the south.

To reach the trailhead, take NM 522 north of Taos 40 miles to NM 196 at Costilla. Turn right on this paved then all-weather gravel road. Seventeen miles from NM 522, at the Carson National Forest

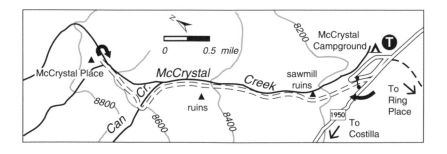

The ranch house at McCrystal Place

boundary, the road becomes FR 1950. Continue about 20 miles to McCrystal Campground. Park off the road near the campground entrance.

From the campground entrance, walk west along FR 1950 for about 0.25 mile to a dirt road angling to the northwest, parallel to the campground road, which is just on the other side of a fence. Bear right, pass through a gate, and stroll through the shady pine forest, watching for tassel-eared squirrels and part of a domestic bison herd run from the nearby Ring Place. After about a mile, the trail meets up with McCrystal Creek to the right. The trail now parallels the creek, passing the large ruins of a sawmill along the way.

At mile 1.5, the road enters a large marshy meadow. A bit farther on, pass a stone foundation to the right and the remains of a wooden structure on the left. At mile 2.6, the road swings to the west to parallel Can Creek. The road heads west for 0.25 mile before bearing right and crossing Can Creek. Descend for several hundred yards before arriving in the meadow surrounding the McCrystal Place.

In a few minutes, reach the large main house and several smaller structures of the ranch. The buildings are fragile and dangerous: stay out. Explore around the ranch and enjoy the view down the valley to the mountains beyond, then return to the trailhead by the same route.

22 NORTH PONIL CREEK

Managed by: Carson National Forest, Valle Vidal Unit, Questa Ranger District
Distance: 8 miles, day hike
Elevation range: 7,750 to 8,000 feet
Elevation gain: 300 feet
Difficulty: easy
Seasons: late May to late October
Water: North Ponil Creek
Maps: USGS Van Bremmer Park and Abreu Canyon 7.5' quadrangles
Interesting features: scenic meadow, ghost town

Walking the long, flower-laced meadow beside North Ponil Creek is a delightful trip back in time a hundred years. The small valley is much like it was before lumbermen pushed a railroad up its serene grasslands, but the traces of human use are still much in evidence. The Cimarron and Northwestern Railway traveled 22 miles from the town of Cimarron into the mountains to Ponil Park, the broadest part of the meadow, which soon became a bustling railroad and lumber town. The railroad connected Ponil Park, the center of operations in the woods, to a series of lumber camps in the canyon below. Perhaps as many as two hundred people lived there in 1910, working the rails, in the sawmills, or as lumbermen. The surrounding forest never provided as much timber for mine supports and railroad ties as the company had anticipated, so the line was torn up in 1921.

To reach the trailhead, take NM 522 north of Taos 40 miles to NM 196 at Costilla. Turn right on this paved then all-weather gravel road. Seventeen miles from NM 522, at the Carson National Forest boundary, the road becomes FR 1950. Continue about 21 miles to park at an information board 1.5 miles beyond McCrystal Campground.

Begin hiking on the south (right) side of the road on a double track behind a "Road Closed" sign. The track leads down canyon, parallel to the diminutive North Ponil Creek. In several hundred yards, pass

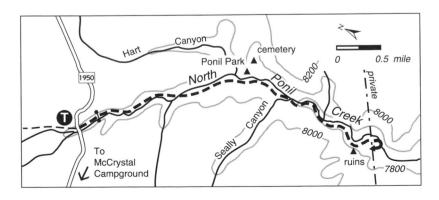

around a gate and continue down the wide meadow. Throughout the summer, hikers will be accompanied by the buzz of dozens of broad-tailed hummingbirds as they visit scarlet Southwest penstemons and lavender New Mexico penstemons.

After 1.5 miles, the trail crosses the stream and follows the boundary of the pine forest on the west side of the valley. At mile 2.1, Hart Canyon joins the North Ponil valley from the left. Ruins of the old town are visible across North Ponil Creek. Continue down the west side of the valley, passing a small railroad trestle and then two cabin ruins. Here the trail parallels the railroad. After Seally Canyon enters from the right, the trail is on top of the railroad grade and rotting ties are found along the route. Continue to walk on the old railroad for another mile until reaching a standing chimney and fireplace in perfect condition. Just beyond, the trail reaches a fence and private land. Turn around and return on the same trail.

On the return trip, cross to the east side of the valley at the first cabin ruins. Look for at least a dozen ruins and a small cemetery. An interesting raised railbed follows the creek, and a stack of firewood appears ready for the return of people to the park. Please respect these reminders of the past and leave them undisturbed. After enjoying the town, continue back up North Ponil Creek 2 miles to the trailhead.

Raised log rail bed at Ponil Park

Jemez Mountains and Bandelier National Monument

Continental Divide Trail marker on the Ojitos Canyon Trail

23 TENT ROCK CANYON TRAILS

Managed by: Bureau of Land Management, Albuquerque District
Distance: 3 miles, day hike
Elevation range: 5,800 to 6,200 feet
Elevation gain: 400 feet
Difficulty: easy
Seasons: mid-March through November
Water: carry water
Map: USGS Cañada 7.5' quadrangle
Interesting features: very narrow canyon, strange-shaped rocks

Tent Rock Canyon is a narrow slice through some tuff ejected from small volcanoes at the edge of the massive Jemez Volcano. In places the walls of the canyon are 200 feet high, but a child's arms can span the entire width. The canyon takes its name from the surrounding weird towers of tuff capped by harder, more erosion-resistant rocks. The cap rocks offer some protection to the crumbly tuff directly beneath, resulting in a hoard of conical spires roughly shaped like tepees. Two trails lead into the wonderland, one along the base of the cliffs, another into the canyon.

Take I 25 south from Santa Fe or north from Albuquerque to the Cochiti exit, number 264. Go west on NM 16 for about 8 miles to a T intersection. Turn right onto NM 22, heading for Cochiti Dam. Go past the spillway and, at the base of the dam, turn left with NM 22 as it

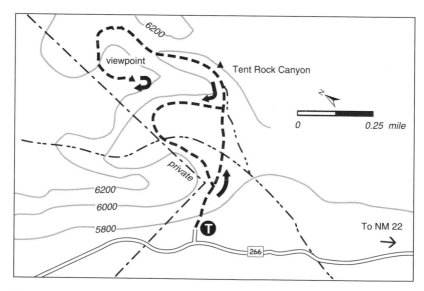

Tepee-shaped tent rocks along upper Tent Rock Canyon

heads toward Cochiti Pueblo. In 1.8 miles, at the end of NM 22, turn right onto FR 266. This dirt road is bumpy but passable to any vehicle. At 4.8 miles, turn right at the Bureau of Land Management (BLM) sign for Tent Rocks. Park in the small lot on the right.

Begin hiking the Tent Rock Canyon Trail at the BLM parking area. Follow the sandy trail, marked with National Recreation Trail sign-posts, about 100 yards to a junction and bear right. A bit less than 0.5 mile from the start, the trail leads into an arroyo. Bear left and walk up the sandy bottom into a narrowing canyon. Just before reaching the mouth of the canyon, the trail splits; the left fork is the cliff trail, but for now go right into the canyon.

The trail passes between high walls of banded volcanic deposits as the canyon alternates between narrow and open sections. Short stretches are a squeeze for an adult with a daypack. At one point hikers must crawl under a boulder to continue, but this only adds to the fun.

At mile 1.2, a primitive trail continues 0.25 mile to a viewpoint above, climbing the steep slope on loose rock. From the viewpoint, backtrack to the mouth of the canyon. Just outside the canyon, turn right onto the cliff route and climb steeply out of the arroyo. After 200 yards, drop into a broad amphitheater surrounded by banded cliffs. The trail follows the base of the cliffs, passing a cave that shows signs of use by Anasazi/Pueblo people. Just past the cave, descend into a narrow arroyo. At the bottom, turn left and walk down the arroyo. In 100 yards, cross a larger arroyo and continue as the trail skirts the base of the western side of the amphitheater to the parking area.

2A RED DOT AND BLUE DOT TRAILS

Managed by: Los Alamos County
Distance: 8 miles, day hike
Elevation range: 5,500 to 6,400 feet
Elevation gain: 900 feet
Difficulty: moderate
Seasons: all year
Water: Pajarito Springs
Map: USGS White Rock 7.5' quadrangle
Interesting features: White Rock Canyon, Rio Grande, petroglyphs, springs

White Rock Canyon has been carved by the Rio Grande through thick lava flows emanating from the volcanoes of the Cerros del Rio volcanic field to the east. Two spectacular trails, unimaginatively named for the color of painted circles that mark the routes, lead into the canyon. The trails are stair-step affairs, descending from successive blocks of lava that slumped from the cliffs as the Rio Grande wore its way down through the rocks. These are ancient trails used by Anasazi/Pueblo people to travel from villages to agricultural fields within the canyon.

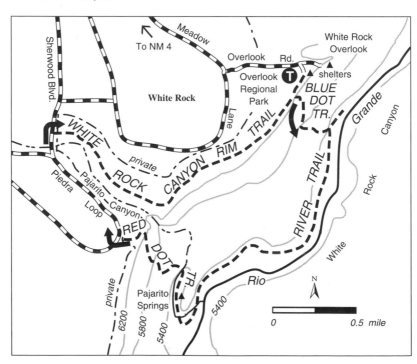

From Santa Fe, go north on US 84/285 for 12 miles to NM 502 and bear left. Continue 8 miles and bear right onto NM 4 to White Rock. On the north edge of town, turn left onto Rover Boulevard. Make the first left onto Meadow Lane, traveling 0.7 mile to the entrance to Overlook Regional Park. Turn left and continue past several athletic fields to a gravel road to the right, which leads to two picnic shelters. Park near the shelters. Note that the park closes at 10:00 P.M.

The trailhead is unmarked and difficult to find. From the picnic shelters, climb over a vehicle barrier and walk south, picking up the trail nearest the rim of White Rock Canyon. In about 150 yards, the Blue Dot Trail starts at a gap in a fence. Turn left, dropping through a cleft in the rim, and begin the quick descent to the Rio Grande. From here the trail is much easier to follow: look for the blue dots painted on the rocks. Dropping from the topmost lava flow, the trail turns many tight switchbacks and crosses two broad benches. Just above the river, the trail enters a juniper woodland and becomes soggy from a few of the many springs that discharge into the river within the canyon.

At a trail junction near the river, the left spur leads in 0.25 mile to a sandy beach at streamside. To continue on the loop, turn right onto the

Snow-covered White Rock Canyon from the Blue Dot Trail

River Trail, which begins with a long, sandy stretch. As the river comes in view again, the trail is squeezed between the river and a long ridge. Follow the trail around the end of the ridge, climbing to a bench covered with river cobbles.

After the trail again drops back to river level, cross the flow from Pajarito Springs using one of the many possible routes. Pick up the Red Dot Trail on the other side, turn right, and head up the small stream. The trail recrosses the stream within a couple hundred feet. With the stream to the left, watch to the right for a steep trail and climb over a ridge. In a few minutes, reach the pools of Pajarito Springs. This is a good place to rest before the long climb out of the canyon.

The trail from the springs is very steep. On the way up, take your mind off the hard work by enjoying the expanding view and by watching for elaborate petroglyphs on the rocks. About halfway up, the trail crosses a level bench, then completes the steep route to the rim. Out of the canyon, turn left and follow the trail to Piedra Loop.

To return to Overlook Park, turn right on Piedra Loop and walk about 0.5 mile to Sherwood Boulevard. Turn right, then in 200 yards, turn right again at a gate on a dirt road where a small sign to the right marks the beginning of the White Rock Canyon Rim Trail. Follow the Rim Trail as it winds through the juniper woodlands of the mesa top. Many intersecting trails lead off in all directions; stay on the main route by heading generally east, keeping Pajarito Canyon on the right and White Rock Canyon ahead. After 1 mile on the Rim Trail, reach the edge of White Rock Canyon and bear left. Follow the trail along the canyon rim back to Overlook Park.

25 FRIJOLES CANYON

Managed by: Bandelier National Monument
Distance: 7 miles one-way, day hike
Elevation range: 6,100 to 7,600 feet
Elevation gain: 1,500-foot descent
Difficulty: easy
Seasons: mid-March through mid-November
Water: Rio Frijoles
Maps: USGS Frijoles 7.5' quadrangle; Trails Illustrated Bandelier National Monument
Interesting features: wildlife, cliff dwellings, running water, picturesque canyon

Frijoles Canyon has been used as a route into the Jemez Mountains for centuries, first by the Anasazi residents in the lower canyon, then by their Pueblo descendants. Today the canyon is a quiet, sheltered

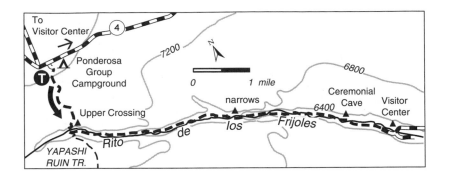

place with year-round running water, making it a haven for wildlife. Elk are commonly spotted on the plateau above the canyon floor; mule deer are plentiful in the canyon itself. The entire canyon is shady, even in mid-summer. The upper canyon supports tall Douglas fir, which gives way to Ponderosa pine as the canyon cuts deeper into the rocks. Although the lower end of Frijoles receives heavy visitation, the upper canyon sees few hikers.

This one-way, downhill hike requires setting up a short shuttle. Park a vehicle at the Bandelier Visitor Center, located off NM 4 10 miles west of White Rock. Return to the park entrance and turn left onto NM 4. Continue 6 miles to the Ponderosa Group Campground and park at the well-marked trailhead heading for Upper Crossing.

Begin hiking downhill on a trail that soon joins a fire road entering from the right. Follow the signs to Upper Crossing at a minor intersection at mile 0.4, then enter the Bandelier Wilderness just above the edge of Frijoles Canyon. The trail drops 400 feet on several steep switchbacks to reach the bottom of Frijoles Canyon at mile 1.5. Cross the creek on a log bridge and immediately come to a three-way trail junction. Turn left onto the Frijoles Canyon Trail, heading toward the Visitor Center and paralleling the Rito de los Frijoles. The trail stays close to the stream with several crossings on log bridges.

About 3.5 miles from the start, an interesting side canyon enters from the left. Just after this junction, walk through the narrows of Frijoles Canyon where the walls are only a dozen feet apart.

The easy shaded stroll continues until another narrow section of canyon forces the trail up and over a steep ridge. Cliff dwellings appear in the canyon wall to the left, but hikers must stay on the trail. About 6 miles from the start, the trail meets the Ceremonial Cave Trail coming up from the Visitor Center. Ceremonial Cave is 140 feet above the canyon floor, reached via several long ladders, and is a worthwhile side trip. Continue on the gravel path to the parking area near the Visitor Center.

Many trails in Bandelier National Monument show signs of long use dating back to the Anasazi.

26   YAPASHI RUINS

Managed by: Bandelier National Monument
Distance: 13 miles, day hike or backpack
Elevation range: 6,000 to 7,400 feet
Elevation gain: 1,800 feet
Difficulty: strenuous
Seasons: mid-April to October
Water: Rio Frijoles, Upper Alamo Crossing, Capulin Canyon
Maps: USGS Frijoles 7.5' quadrangle, Trails Illustrated Bandelier National Monument
Interesting features: stunning views, large junipers, Anasazi ruins

The best way to see a large portion of the Bandelier backcountry is to set up a short shuttle and hike one-way from Upper Crossing to the

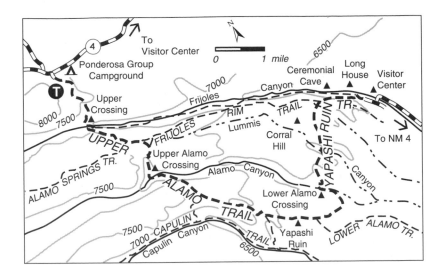

Visitor Center via the Upper Alamo Trail. Park a vehicle at the Bandelier Visitor Center, return to the park entrance, and turn left onto NM 4. Continue 6 miles to the Ponderosa Group Campground and park at the well-marked trailhead heading for Upper Crossing.

In the Bandelier backcountry, canyons are cut between finger-like mesas radiating from the hand of the Jemez Mountains. This hike drops into and out of three steep canyons, accumulating an elevation gain of almost 2,000 feet. The roughest, steepest climb is at Lower Alamo Crossing near the end of the hike. This long trek invites an overnight stay. No camping is permitted in upper Alamo or Frijoles canyons, and no fires are allowed in the backcountry: use only gas stoves for cooking. Yapashi Ruin is one of the largest pueblos on the Pajarito Plateau. Hikers will find standing tuff-block walls, kiva depressions, and red and brown pottery scattered throughout the ruin. To protect this ancient structure, stay off the walls and kiva and leave potsherds where they are found. This trail can be very hot in summer, with little shade available for long stretches.

Begin hiking on a trail and fire road through the open ponderosa pine forest. Bear right at an intersection about 0.25 mile from the start. About a mile from the start, drop into the head of a small drainage and follow a series of steep switchbacks to the Upper Crossing of Rito de los Frijoles and the cool shady bottom of the canyon.

After crossing the small stream on a log bridge, follow the trail a hundred feet to a junction. Bear left then right to follow the trail to Yapashi Ruin, which angles up the south slope of the canyon. (The Frijoles Canyon Trail also goes to the left, but it stays in the canyon bottom.) Climb out of the canyon on several switchbacks, reaching the top at mile 2. The low plant growth and tall standing snags on the mesa are evidence this area was hard hit by the 1977 La Mesa fire. After the trail drops into and out of a small drainage, bear left at the junction with the Alamo Springs Trail. At the next intersection at mile 3.1, bear right as the Frijoles Rim Trail goes left and pass another branch of that trail angling back to the left in a few hundred yards.

The route now drops slowly into Upper Alamo Canyon via a small side drainage. The trail reaches Alamo Canyon directly below several small, colorful tent rocks halfway up the canyon wall. Cross Alamo Creek at a delightful spot about 4 miles from the start. The trail turns downstream in the canyon bottom for 0.25 mile before climbing to the mesa above. Bear left at the junction with a trail marked for Capulin Canyon. From here the trail descends through open pine forest along a small drainage. At mile 6.1, the trail meets the edge of an escarpment, offering more long-range views to the east. Drop down several rocky switchbacks before bearing left at another trail junction at mile 7.3. The trail to the right leads to water and fine campsites in Capulin Canyon.

Continue east on the top of a ridge where at first the trail is confused by a network of side trails. Gradually the main trail becomes easy to follow. About 0.5 mile beyond the side trail leading to Capulin Canyon, reach the low mounds of Yapashi Ruin. Explore around the perimeter of the ruins before continuing down the trail.

From Yapashi, follow the ridge top before dropping down into and out of a small canyon. While traveling through open juniper pine woodland, pass the junction with the Lower Alamo Trail to the right. Climb a low ridge, then drop 500 feet to Lower Alamo Crossing. The canyon

Alamo Canyon is carved into the Pajarito Plateau.

bottom is shaded by pines and box elders, with flowing water in the spring. Make a short hitch west up the canyon bottom under towering orange cliffs. The staircase climb to the next mesa is the hottest, toughest part of the hike, but shady ponderosa pines dot the rim.

Heading north toward Frijoles Canyon, cross a small drainage, then the larger Lummis Canyon. Beyond the foot of Corral Hill, make one last climb to the edge of Frijoles Canyon. About 12 miles from the start, meet the Frijoles Rim Trail and bear right. (For those doing a loop hike, turn left; it is 6.5 miles back to the trailhead.) In a few hundred feet, enjoy views into Frijoles Canyon and look across the canyon for the ladders to Ceremonial Cave. The trail now angles down the south wall of Frijoles Canyon, offering views of Long House along the way, and soon reaches the trailhead near the Visitor Center.

27 TYUONYI OVERLOOK TRAIL

Managed by: Bandelier National Monument
Distance: 2 miles, day hike
Elevation range: 6,600 to 6,700 feet
Elevation gain: 100 feet
Difficulty: easy
Seasons: all year
Water: carry water
Maps: USGS Frijoles 7.5' quadrangle, Trails Illustrated Bandelier National Monument
Interesting features: overhead view of large Anasazi pueblo ruin

Most visitors to Bandelier National Monument stay on the floor of Frijoles Canyon to tour the main ruin, Tyuonyi, but the view of the ruin from above gives a better sense of what the canyon was like during

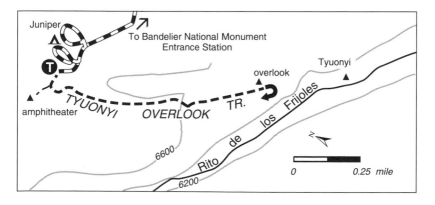

Frijoles Canyon and Tyuonyi ruin from the end of the Overlook Trail

the Anasazi occupation 500 years ago. Perched on the peaceful canyon rim 400 feet above the village, one can easily imagine the canyon bustling with the sights and sounds of six hundred Anasazi. Visit the ruin first, then take the overlook trail for another perspective.

The entrance to Bandelier National Monument is located on NM 4, 13 miles west of the intersection of NM 502 and NM 4 near Los Alamos. The trailhead for the Tyuonyi Overlook Trail is at the end of the Juniper Campground road, which is the first right-hand turn after passing through the entrance to the monument. Park in the large lot for the amphitheater.

Begin hiking toward the amphitheater at the west end of the parking lot. At the bottom of the stairs, turn left onto the Tyuonyi Overlook Trail. Pass under tall ponderosa pines before entering the juniper woodland beyond. In spring, wildflowers are found among the rocks as in a rock garden. Spring is also a good time for bird watching, with flocks of piñon jays, robins, and evening grosbeaks flitting through the trees. Stay on the wide, main trail.

After 0.5 mile, the trail bears left to parallel the rim of Frijoles Canyon. Views across the canyon take in the sloping walls of Bandelier tuff, or welded volcanic ash. To the west, the Jemez Mountains, the remains of the volcano that produced the tuff, make up the skyline. Drop gradually on the now rocky trail to the viewpoint about a mile from the start. Find a quiet spot to enjoy the view of the canyon and the ruin below and the play of ravens overhead. Return to the trailhead by the same route.

28 EAST FORK OF THE JEMEZ RIVER

Managed by: Santa Fe National Forest, Jemez National Recreation Area, Jemez Ranger District
Distance: 6 miles one way, day hike
Elevation range: 8,000 to 8,600 feet
Elevation gain: 600 feet
Difficulty: easy
Seasons: mid-April through November
Water: East Fork of the Jemez River
Map: USGS Redondo Peak 7.5' quadrangle
Interesting features: inside a dormant volcano, fishing, wildlife, mountain meadows

In contrast to the many rugged hikes found in New Mexico, a stroll along the East Fork is an easy, relaxing walk. The high-country stream flows within a rocky canyon in a deep conifer forest, yet the river meanders through a series of open meadows filled in summer with a riot of wildflowers. The canyon is home to mountain wildlife,

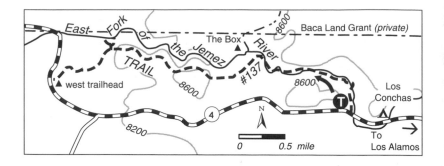

including mule deer, elk, bobcat, raccoon, and porcupine; birdsong fills the air at any time of day. The East Fork is well-stocked with rainbow trout, and the most enjoyable hikes along the river include stops at the large pools for a bit of angling.

To set up a shuttle for a one-way hike, leave a car at the U.S. Forest Service East Fork Trailhead. From San Ysidro on NM 44, travel north on NM 4, passing through Jemez Springs and past the intersection with NM 126. The well-marked trailhead is about 5 miles from NM 126. From Los Alamos, go west on NM 501 to NM 4. Turn right and continue for 21 miles to the parking area. Next, drive 3.5 miles east on NM 4 to the Las Conchas Trailhead, which is 0.25 mile west of the Las Conchas Picnic Area.

At the trailhead, the route descends wooden stairs from the parking lot to river level. Follow the trail as it heads downstream past tall cliffs of volcanic rock and through alternating patches of forest and meadow. In the first 0.5 mile, make five stream crossings on log bridges. Nice campsites are located along the river after the fourth bridge and beyond.

The trail reaches the head of the East Fork Box in 2 miles. Here the main trail turns left and climbs to the canyon rim, but first take the short spur trail that leads along the river to views of the Box, a wild section of canyon. The main trail ascends on gentle switchbacks, then parallels the canyon on the mesa above. Continue west along the rim, parallel to a logging road that stays to the left. Much of this section of trail is a pleasant walk through open ponderosa pine forest.

At mile 4, a spur trail to the right descends again to the river. This trail branches about halfway down, the right fork dropping steeply to the bottom of the Box—a delightful and popular lunch stop—and the left fork leading to a trail along the river. Take both spurs and climb back to the main trail.

The last mile of trail descends slowly through a recently logged pine stand. Near the end, the trail merges with a wide logging road, marked as a ski trail with blue diamonds. Reach the west trailhead about 5 miles from Las Conchas or 6 miles including the side trip to the river.

Log bridge across the East Fork of the Jemez River

29 RITO DE LAS PERCHAS LOOP

Managed by: Santa Fe National Forest, San Pedro Parks Wilderness, Cuba
    Ranger District
Distance: 13.5 miles, backpack
Elevation range: 9,400 to 10,400 feet
Elevation gain: 1,800 feet
Difficulty: moderate
Seasons: late June through late September
Water: Rito de las Perchas, Rio de las Vacas
Maps: USGS Nacimiento Peak 7.5' quadrangle, USFS San Pedro Parks
    Wilderness
Interesting features: unique plateau scenery, wildlife, solitude, good fishing

    The San Pedro Parks Wilderness sits on a high granite plateau at
the northwestern edge of the Jemez Mountains. The parks average
9,500 feet in elevation. Damp granitic soils produce extensive meadows
interrupted by open stands of fir and spruce, offering an expansive
feeling not often found high in the mountains. Although the hiking is

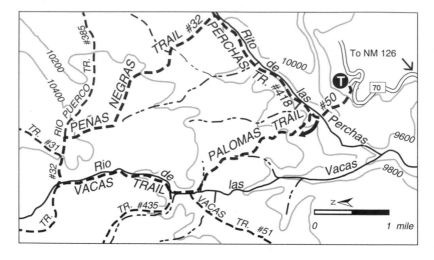

easy, this unique landscape is little known and sees few visitors. It is the perfect summer escape from the crowds. The extensive network of trails invites a couple days of exploration.

Elk and bear are frequently spotted in the meadows, and native Rio Grande cutthroat trout swim the clear waters of the Rio de las Vacas, Rito de las Perchas, and Clear Creek. Because of the high elevation, snow lingers well into June and trails can be quite soggy until early July. Hikers should bring their best hiking boots and extra pairs of socks. Note that the trails often cross open bogs and can be difficult to follow; watch for wooden posts that mark the way.

Reach the San Pedro Parks via NM 126 out of Cuba or the village of La Cueva (north of Albuquerque via NM 44 and NM 4). Take NM 126 about 30 miles from La Cueva, most of which is unpaved, but is passable to high-clearance vehicles except in winter and after heavy rains. From Cuba, take NM 126 about 6 miles; all but the last 0.5 mile is paved. Turn onto FR 70, heading north. In 3 miles, pass the parking for Trail No. 51 and continue on the winding-but-good gravel road another 10 miles. Park on the left at the large wilderness trailhead.

From the trailhead, walk uphill on the Palomas Trail No. 50. This climb is the steepest on the hike, a 500-foot ascent over the first mile. Cross the wilderness boundary shortly before topping out on the ridge, then make a straight drop to the Rito de las Perchas. The trail crosses the creek, then heads upstream a hundred feet to intersect the Perchas Trail No. 418, the return route for this loop. Turn left to stay on Trail No. 50, heading across a meadow toward the Rio de las Vacas.

Begin another climb up a small drainage. At the top, follow stout trail markers across a small meadow. The trail now bears left and descends to a soupy meadow of tall grasses before dropping into the valley of the Las Vacas. At a prominent intersection, continue straight onto the Vacas Trail No. 51. In 0.5 mile, cross the Las Vacas and pass the Anastacio Trail No. 435. At mile 5.8, bear right and continue up the valley, which is now a wide meadow with a small stream meandering through it. Along the edges of the valley are numerous campsites with memorable views.

Near mile 8, at the junction with the Peñas Negras Trail No. 32, turn right and climb a short drainage to a saddle. On top of the saddle, pass the Rio Capulin Trail No. 31 to the left. At the junction with the Rio Puerco Trail No. 385, turn right to continue on the Peñas Negras Trail, which now heads southeast. Walk across a high plateau, then descend along a small meadow. About 3 miles from the Rio de las Vacas, pass the Vega Redonda Trail No. 43 on the left. In another 0.5 mile, come to the Rito de las Perchas and more excellent campsites in wide meadows near the very edge of the plateau.

Near the crossing of the Las Perchas, turn right onto the Perchas Trail No. 418. Parallel the creek downstream through more wet meadows. In 2.5 miles, intersect the Palomas Trail at the junction noted before. Cross the stream on the Palomas Trail, climb the steep hill, then enjoy the descent back to the trailhead.

Most trails in the San Pedro Parks Wilderness parallel streams.

30   RIM VISTA TRAIL

Managed by: Carson National Forest, Canjilon Ranger District
Distance: 4.5 miles, day hike
Elevation range: 6,700 to 7,900 feet
Elevation gain: 1,200 feet
Difficulty: moderate
Seasons: March to December
Water: carry water
Map: USGS Echo Amphitheater 7.5' quadrangle
Interesting features: outstanding view of red-rock country

The sedimentary rock layers of the Colorado Plateau create grand scenery from Utah to New Mexico. The rocks tell the story of shallow seas with dinosaurs roaming the shorelines, of shallow freshwater lakes, and a massive sand dune desert rivaling the modern Sahara. Nowhere are these rocks more colorfully displayed than from the edge of the Mesa de los Viejos and an overlook simply called Rim Vista. The hike to the vista climbs from the red mudstones of the Chinle Formation to the top of the Dakota sandstone, a climb through time of almost 100 million years. Little shade is available on this route, making it ideal in spring, fall, or winter, but it is to be avoided in summer.

From Española, travel north on US 84 about 37 miles to FR 151, about 1 mile past the USFS Ghost Ranch Visitor Center. Turn left onto FR 151, a graded gravel road suited for all vehicles in dry weather. Seven-tenths of a mile from the highway, turn right onto a dirt track, which is signed for the Rim Vista Trail. In 0.2 mile, bear right at a Y intersection and park at the trailhead in another 0.1 mile.

Head west on Trail No. 15, immediately dropping into and out of a small arroyo. Climb around the end of a ridge to the top, passing in 0.2 mile a small knife-edge ridge with views to the right of swirling patterns in the Entrada sandstone. Continue a steeper climb on the south flank of the ridge. Beyond, blue diamonds mark the wide trail as it climbs a rocky section of slope through juniper-piñon woodland.

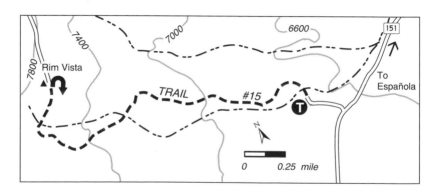

Mesozoic Period rocks on the cliffs above Ghost Ranch as seen from Rim Vista

As the trail flattens out, climb a broad ridge dotted with sagebrush and large piñon pines. At mile 1.2, the trail swings south, then west again. In another mile, the gradual slope ends as the trail climbs a broad bench, then turns north to parallel the cliff of Dakota sandstone above. The view becomes more grand with each step, culminating at the vista at mile 2.2. On the mesa top, pick a rock to sit on and take a well-deserved break to enjoy the long-distance views. From the vista point, the rocks of Ghost Ranch, Abiquiu Lake, the Jemez Mountains, and the Sangre de Cristo Range are in view. Return to the trailhead by the same route.

31 OJITOS CANYON TRAIL

Managed by: Santa Fe National Forest, Rio Chama Wilderness, Coyote
    Ranger District
Distance: 12 miles, day hike or backpack
Elevation range: 6,350 to 8,100 feet
Elevation gain: 1,900 feet
Difficulty: moderate
Seasons: mid-March to November
Water: intermittent in Ojitos Creek, carry water
Map: USGS Laguna Peak 7.5' quadrangle
Interesting features: colorful cliffs, secluded backcountry camping

A trip into Ojitos Canyon is a hiker's hike, a trip taken more for the sheer joy of walking and being in the backcountry than to reach a

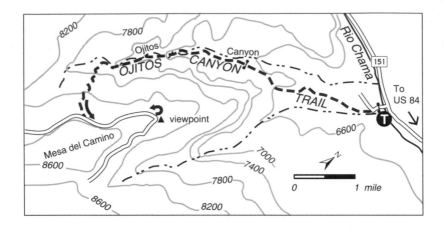

destination. The trail is one of northern New Mexico's only completed sections of the Continental Divide Trail. It follows Ojitos Canyon through the colorful cliffs of Mesozoic rocks in the little-used Rio Chama Wilderness. The trail is well marked with Continental Divide Trail markers. Backcountry campsites are abundant in the canyon and near the trail's end on Mesa del Camino. A trickle of water will be found in the stream most of the year. Watch for chunks of white quartz, gypsum, and petrified wood, all common in the red Chinle mudstones along the first 2 miles of the trail.

From Española, travel north on US 84 about 37 miles to FR 151, about 1 mile past the USFS Ghost Ranch Visitor Center. Turn left onto FR 151, a dirt road suited for all vehicles in dry weather. Continue about 8.5 miles to Skull Bridge on the Rio Chama and park.

Cross the Rio Chama on the bridge and continue through a gate on the dirt road heading south. In 200 yards, the road swings west as the trail continues straight; look for pointed posts inscribed with the Continental Divide Trail symbol. After entering the Rio Chama Wilderness, the trail passes along the wide mouth of Ojitos Canyon through open sagebrush country backed by red, tan, and yellow cliffs. Follow the trail as it turns left, entering a gap, then proceed around a mudstone mesa and over a low saddle before dropping back into the main canyon.

Immediately after passing through another hikers' gate at mile 2.1, bear right and watch for the next trail marker. The path now closely follows the canyon bottom, where running water is found most of the year. Much of the trail follows the route of an abandoned *acequia*, and metal flumes from the old ditch can be found at several stream crossings.

At mile 4.5, while on the east bank of the stream, the trail leaves the canyon bottom and begins to climb the wall of Mesa del Camino on a long series of steep switchbacks. Here the trail passes through an open forest of ponderosa pine and Gambel oak, offering views of the Ojitos Basin. About 0.75 mile up the switchbacks, watch for a view through the trees of the canyon country below and of the San Juan Mountains on the distant horizon. Near the top of the climb, the trail leaves the wilderness and reaches a sloping bench at about 8,000 feet. The trail skirts the northwest edge of the bench, ending at a dirt road a couple hundred feet below the flat summit of Mesa del Camino. To the left is a protected campsite. From the end of the trail, hikers can bushwhack straight up to the summit of the mesa or take the more moderate course of following the road to the north about a mile to a saddle that offers excellent views both to the west and east. Return to the trailhead by the same route.

Northwest Plateau and Zuni Mountains

Colorful bedded sedimentary rocks are characteristic of the Northwest Plateau.

32 KITCHEN MESA

Managed by: Ghost Ranch Presbyterian Center
Distance: 5 miles, day hike
Elevation range: 6,500 to 7,100 feet
Elevation gain: 600 feet
Difficulty: easy, except for short climb
Seasons: late April to November
Water: carry water
Map: USGS Ghost Ranch 7.5' quadrangle
Interesting features: red-rock scenery, wide open vistas

The Ghost Ranch area, with its naked red-rock landscape, is more characteristic of northern Arizona or southern Utah than New Mexico. The brick-red mudstones of the Chinle Formation—massive river delta deposits from the age of the early dinosaurs—dominate Ghost Ranch. Above the Chinle are soaring cliffs of yellow-brown Entrada sandstone capped by gray lake deposits of the Todilto Formation. The trip to the top of Kitchen Mesa takes hikers into the heart of this wilderness of stone, leading to breathtaking views of rocks, cliffs, and Abiquiu Lake to the south.

The Kitchen Mesa Trail traverses private land owned by the Ghost Ranch Presbyterian Center, which is very receptive to use of the trail by responsible hikers. Before hitting the trail, hikers must check in at the office and tell the staff of their plans to visit Kitchen Mesa.

From Española, take US 84/285 north. Continue about 40 miles, staying on US 84 when US 285 splits off. About 6 miles past NM 96, turn right onto the gravel road marked for the Ghost Ranch Presbyterian

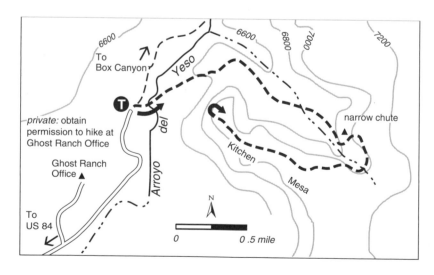

The narrow chute on the way to the top of Kitchen Mesa

Center. (This is not the same as the Ghost Ranch Living Museum, which is about 1.5 miles beyond the Presbyterian Center.) In 1 mile, the road forks; follow the signs left to the office and ask for permission to hike the Kitchen Mesa Trail. Drive back to the fork, turn left, and continue slowly through the center. About 0.5 mile from the office, park in a large area just before a "No Vehicles Beyond This Point" sign.

The Kitchen Mesa Trail is marked with blue coffee cans. Find the first can by walking up the road from the parking area for about 100 yards, then turn right to cross a small stream. Climb to the bluff above the stream and walk the easy-to-follow trail across a sagebrush flat. Around a small hill, the trail passes in the shadow of Kitchen Mesa 400 feet overhead. Yes, the end of this trail is only 0.25 mile from the beginning!

The trail suddenly climbs and descends a steep, open slope of red Chinle mudstones, then bears right in a broad canyon. At mile 0.7, the trail crosses the canyon bottom, then climbs up the slope on the north side of the canyon. One mile from the start, the trail crosses a slick stretch of loose rock where caution is required. The route climbs steeply up the rocks; follow the blue cans, painted blue arrows, and the path worn into the rocks. On the last section of the ascent, hikers must be able to boost themselves up through a fissure in the rock to reach the top of the mesa. Fortunately, well-placed hand- and footholds make the short climb easier than it first appears.

Once up the crack, the trail is almost on the mesa top. Bear right and cross the head of an arroyo, then make a final climb. The trail again bears right at the top of the mesa. From the 2-mile point, the trail crosses an eerie, barren white landscape on top of the gypsum lakebeds of the Todilto Formation. Walk to the end of the mesa and enjoy the expansive view. Bright sun and wind can make the last exposed 0.5 mile of trail unpleasant, so retreat to the edge of the junipers to find some shade for lunch or a rest stop. Return to the trailhead by the same route.

33 MESA MONTOSA

Managed by: Ghost Ranch Presbyterian Center; Carson National Forest, Canjilon Ranger District
Distance: 10 miles, day hike
Elevation range: 6,500 to 7,850 feet
Elevation gain: 1,800 feet
Difficulty: moderate
Seasons: March to November
Water: carry water
Map: USGS Ghost Ranch 7.5' quadrangle
Interesting features: red-rock cliffs, fossils, spectacular box canyon and pour off

Mesa Montosa is part of the northern boundary of the basin of Mesozoic rocks surrounding the Rio Chama. On the way to the mesa top, a short side trip leads to Box Canyon. The spur dead-ends at a pour off—a normally dry waterfall—about 200 feet high and with a noticeable overhang. In the box, hikers are surrounded by yellow rock cliffs on all sides. Throughout late fall to early spring, seeps in the cliff face are frozen, decorating the alcove with pillars of ice. Beyond Box Canyon, the trail climbs through time as well as altitude beginning with Jurassic Entrada sandstone, which is the cliff-forming rock of the canyon walls. The yellow, green, and purple muds of the Morrison Formation

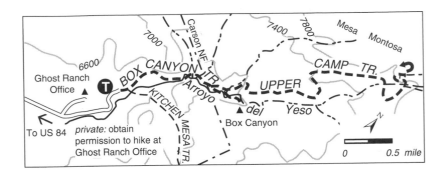

form a broad bench above the cliffs. Finally, the trail climbs the next cliff, the Cretaceous Dakota sandstone.

This hike begins on the private Ghost Ranch Presbyterian Center at the same trailhead as the Kitchen Mesa hike. Follow the same directions for access and securing permission to hike as listed for the Kitchen Mesa Trail (hike No. 32).

From the parking area, begin walking on the road marked for Kitchen Mesa and Box Canyon. In a hundred feet, the Kitchen Mesa Trail turns right. Continue straight and follow the road as it skirts the base of a monolith of Entrada sandstone. Just after crossing an irrigation ditch, take the right fork, dropping down along the bottom of Arroyo del Yeso.

Heading upstream on a wide trail, cross under a flume, which is part of the old irrigation system for the ranch below. The trail now stays close to the stream, crossing it many times in the shade of the cottonwoods. At a trail junction at mile 1.2, take the right fork marked for Box Canyon. After several minutes, come to a small oasis where two canyons meet and enjoy the small pools and waterfalls. Continue up the main canyon for 200 yards to the massive alcove and the high pour off. The last section of trail requires a bit of scrambling over the rocks.

After enjoying the alcove, backtrack to the trail junction noted before. Turn right onto the Upper Camp Trail. The trail climbs above the canyon floor before dropping into a side canyon. The trail climbs steeply out of the canyon to a viewpoint overlooking Box Canyon. Crossing a sagebrush flat, the trail levels for 0.5 mile before climbing to another bench. On the bench, the trail swings west before climbing up a small drainage, which is easy to miss. The trail swings back to the east, now paralleling the high cliff of brown Dakota sandstone to the left.

At mile 4.4, the trail again crosses the Arroyo del Yeso before climbing around a knoll. This steep section of trail offers great views of the Dakota cliff winding off to the west. Reach a low saddle and begin dropping to upper Arroyo del Yeso. Before reaching the canyon bottom, bear left on a faint trail that crosses the canyon and climbs the opposite canyon wall on an old road. Several branches of the trail climb the hill: select any one. The old road contours around a point of Mesa Montosa, then climbs to the mesa top. Look for a road to the right that

Ice columns at the head of Box Canyon in early spring

leads to the point of the mesa and long-distance views of the Jemez Mountains, the Rio Chama Canyon, and Abiquiu Lake. After enjoying the view, return by the same route.

34 NAVAJO PEAK

Managed by: Santa Fe National Forest, Coyote Ranger District, Bureau of Land Management, Taos Resource Area
Distance: 11 miles, day hike or backpack
Elevation range: 6,400 to 7,700 feet
Elevation gain: 2,000 feet
Difficulty: moderate
Seasons: May to October
Water: Rio Cebolla
Map: USGS Navajo Peak 7.5' quadrangle
Interesting features: great canyon scenery, good fishing, solitude

As the highest point on the edge of a broad mesa, Navajo Peak is more accurately described as a summit. Regardless of its label, the point nonetheless offers fine views of the canyon of the Rio Chama, the largest tributary to the Rio Grande in New Mexico. The canyon walls soar 1,000 feet above the river, banded with yellow Entrada sandstone and orange-stained rocks of the Chinle Formation. The river itself

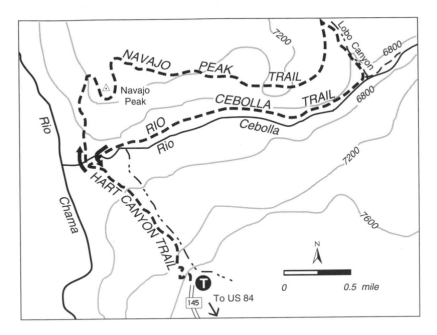

flows through the Rio Chama Wilderness Area, which most visitors access by raft. Fishing for brown and rainbow trout is excellent in both the Chama and the Rio Cebolla. The level ground at the confluence of the two streams holds many fine campsites.

To reach the trailhead, take US 84/285 north from Española about 48 miles to FR 145, about 8 miles north of the Ghost Ranch Living Museum. FR 145 is passable to any vehicle in dry weather but is impassable to all vehicles when wet. In 2.5 miles, pass through private land and continue straight through a gate in the ranch yard. Immediately bear left and continue on FR 145. About 11 miles from the highway, bear right to stay on FR 145 at English Tanks. Continue another 8 miles to the trailhead.

Begin hiking at the mesa edge on the Hart Canyon Trail No. 293. The trail immediately drops down the canyon wall on a series of steep switchbacks, with grand views of the Rio Chama Canyon and the smaller canyon of the Rio Cebolla. After dropping 400 feet in the first 0.5 mile, the grade moderates as the trail crosses a juniper-covered sloping bench to meet the Rio Cebolla at mile 1.6. At a trail junction, continue straight, following the signs for the Navajo Peak Trail. Immediately begin to climb the north wall of the canyon on a broad switchback. The trail ascends steeply up the Entrada cliff where fine patterns of swirling sand are prominent in the rocks. After crossing a broad bench, the trail swings to the west of Navajo Peak before reaching the summit and views of the Rio Chama and Rio Cebolla canyons at mile 2.7.

Mexican hats

From the summit, the trail heads generally east along the rim of the canyon of the Rio Cebolla, crossing rolling hills of thick ponderosa pine. Views north to the southern San Juan Mountains occasionally open up through the trees. Continue for over 2 miles across the mesa to the edge of Lobo Canyon, where the trail descends into the canyon. (This section of trail was scheduled to be improved in 1995.) Bear right with the trail and descend the canyon, meeting the Rio Cebolla at mile 6. Turn right and follow the Rio Cebolla Trail down through a narrow canyon, clambering over many rocks. After 2.5 miles in the canyon, reach the junction with the Hart Canyon Trail at mile 8.5. Turn left onto the Hart Canyon Trail and make the steep climb back to the trailhead.

35 CRUCES BASIN

Managed by: Carson National Forest, Cruces Basin Wilderness Area, Tres Piedras Ranger District
Distance: 8 miles, backpack
Elevation range: 9,250 to 9,900 feet
Elevation gain: 1,200 feet
Difficulty: easy
Seasons: late May through November
Water: Beaver, Diablo, and Cruces creeks
Maps: USGS Toltec Mesa 7.5' quadrangle, USFS Cruces Basin Wilderness
Interesting features: rolling mountain scenery, solitude

The Cruces Basin Wilderness is a small gem in Carson National Forest near the Colorado border. Open meadows, clear streams, long vistas, and bold granite outcrops characterize the high plateau. The long, dusty

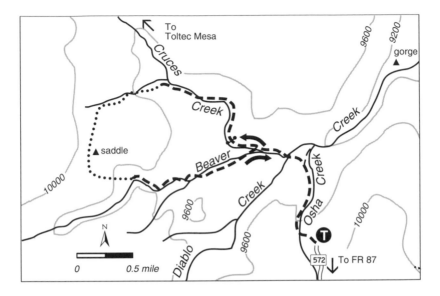

access road discourages most prospective visitors, so hikers are likely to enjoy their trip in relative solitude.

The lack of developed trails helps keep the Cruces Basin Wilderness a lonely place. Hikers must follow informal, fishermen, or game trails. The described loop requires the ability to read a topographic map and find a route through trail-less meadows and forest. Plan to spend several days here exploring from a base camp somewhere along the first half of this route. Campsites and water are plentiful in the valleys of all three creeks. Numerous primitive campsites found along FR 572 just outside the wilderness make excellent overnight stops before a trip into the basin.

Entry to the Cruces Basin Wilderness is from Tres Piedras, about 33 miles west of Taos and 55 miles north of Española. Continue on US 285 north from Tres Piedras about 11 miles to FR 87 and turn left. FR 87 is a long gravel and dirt road passable to any vehicle when dry, but sections of the road can be impassable for days following heavy rains. Follow FR 87 through several junctions, passing FR 87A in 21 miles. A mile beyond FR 87A, turn right onto FR 572, heading uphill. FR 572 is rough and impassable when wet. When the road is dry, a carefully driven car can make the 2 miles to the trailhead.

Begin hiking the well-worn trail heading downhill from behind the wilderness information sign (ignore the fainter trail that follows an old road along the ridge). Drop into the head of Osha Canyon. In a long meadow at mile 1.1, come to a trail junction. Bear left onto the branch leading back into the forest and over a saddle near the end of a ridge.

At the saddle, enjoy wonderful views of the three main streams of the Cruces Basin. To the left is Diablo Creek, straight ahead are Beaver and Cruces creeks. The trail drops on loose rock to the junction of

Diablo and Beaver creeks. Make wet crossings of Diablo Creek, and then, on the other side of a granite outcrop, Beaver Creek. From here the trail is less distinct, frequently disappearing in the wet meadows surrounding the streams. Head up the right side of Beaver Creek, passing some active beaver lodges along the way.

At mile 1.7, the valley splits with Beaver Creek to the left and Cruces Creek to the right. Follow the faint trail past the stream confluence and up Cruces Creek, soon passing through a gate. Just beyond are several shady sites for a base camp. The stream meanders through the broad meadow, turning west and passing beneath a huge wall of granite. Near the base of the rock wall, the trail crosses the stream and parallels the left bank, climbing more steeply. Three miles from the start, around the west side of the granite wall, the trail enters another extensive meadow. At this point, pick up the small stream that meets Cruces Creek in the meadow and follow the smaller stream as it heads west. Watch for blooms of pink shooting stars and bull elephant heads along the banks.

Follow the small stream as it heads uphill and into the forest. In 0.5 mile from Cruces Creek, the stream enters a narrow meadow and soon

Meadows surrounding Beaver Creek in the Cruces Basin Wilderness

forks. Take the left fork, heading south, staying in the meadow. A faint trail near the edge of the trees leads up the meadow toward a saddle. As the trail reaches the marshy saddle, cross a fence line and look for a small, normally dry drainage heading southeast down the other side. Walk parallel to the drainage, dropping steeply through deep forest into the canyon of Beaver Creek. In 0.25 mile, the drainage enters a large meadow with views of the surrounding canyons and ridges. Drop through the meadow to the bottom and meet Beaver Creek. Pick up a trail on the north slope of the canyon that follows Beaver Creek downstream, rounding a massive granite outcrop that has bent the course of the stream to the north.

After a few minutes walking along Beaver Creek, the canyon opens into a broad meadow. Parallel the stream on faint trails down to the junction with Cruces Creek and pick up the trail used before to ascend the valley. Backtrack past the confluence of Diablo and Beaver creeks, then make the moderate climb up Osha Creek to return to the trailhead.

36 DE-NA-ZIN WILDERNESS

Managed by: Bureau of Land Management, De-Na-Zin Wilderness, Farmington District Office
Distance: 4 miles, day hike
Elevation range: 6,200 to 6,350 feet
Elevation gain: 200 feet
Difficulty: easy
Seasons: March through November
Water: carry water
Map: USGS Alamo Mesa East 7.5' quadrangle
Interesting features: badlands topography, strange rocks, isolation

The De-Na-Zin Wilderness area is not as well known as its companion wilderness, the Bisti, but offers six times the land area of similar wild scenery. Rocks deposited in swamps and forests on the edge of an ancient sea have eroded into fascinating shapes. The landscape is filled with lithic mushrooms, chocolate drops, turbans, and goblins. Also abundant within the wilderness are petrified logs, dinosaur bones, and mammal fossils.

No established trails are found within the wilderness, but cross-country travel is easy. Wandering is encouraged, and the following route is only one of many possibilities for exploring. Hikers should be alert for the unmarked boundaries with private inholdings within the wilderness; fences usually mark the boundaries of grazing allotments. Visitors must stay off fragile formations and are prohibited from collecting rocks and fossils.

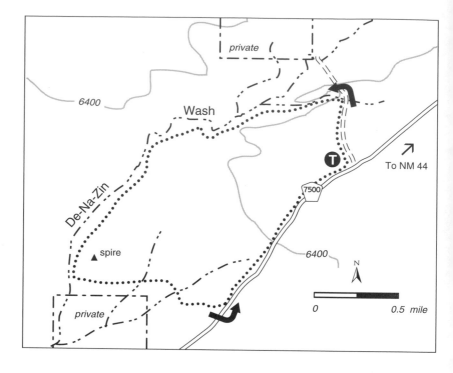

Several access points to the wilderness are found along San Juan County Road 7500. Pick up CR 7500 at Huerfano Trading Post, about 40 miles south of Farmington on NM 44. Turn right (west) onto CR 7500 and drive 12 miles to a parking area on the right.

From the parking area, continue straight on a dirt road heading north. Climb a low hill, then drop gradually to reach an arroyo about 0.4 mile from the start. Turn left into the arroyo and walk in the sandy bottom. The arroyo soon drops into a shallow and narrow canyon. At mile 0.9, the canyon opens up into a broader gorge and at mile 1.2, it intersects the larger De-na-Zin Wash. Turn left to head down the arroyo. Walking is slow in the sand, but there is plenty of scenery to attract the hiker's attention. Continue down the wash, exploring any or all of the interesting side canyons and alcoves found along the way.

After following the convoluted course of the wash for 1.3 miles, watch for a tall spire of rock detached from the cliff to the left. Private land is just downstream, so hikers should turn around here. An alternative is to exit the arroyo and walk to the southeast, parallel to the low cliff on the left, to reach CR 7500 in 1.1 miles, crossing two arroyos along the way. At the road, turn left and walk 1.5 miles back to the trailhead.

Eroded badlands in the De-Na-Zin Wilderness (Mark Nohl photo, courtesy of *New Mexico Magazine*)

37 ALTO MESA LOOP

Managed by: Chaco Canyon National Historical Park
Distance: 5 miles, day hike
Elevation range: 6,100 to 6,400 feet
Elevation gain: 300 feet
Difficulty: moderate
Seasons: all year
Water: carry water
Map: Chaco Canyon National Historical Park brochure
Interesting features: best views of large Chaco ruins, remains of Chaco road system

In a state famous for its abundance of ruins of large Native American villages, Chaco Canyon holds the crown jewels. Visitors to the remains of multiple-story towns scattered along 6 miles of canyon floor are soon struck by the magical, mystical nature of the canyon. For whatever reason, the Anasazi people, ancestors of the modern Pueblo groups living in New Mexico and Arizona, chose this canyon to build villages with hundreds of rooms.

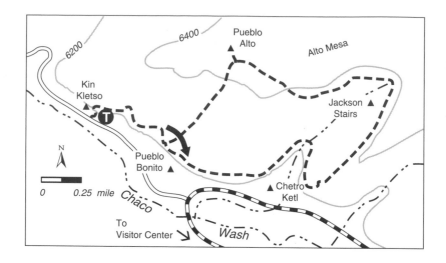

At present, no paved roads lead to Chaco Canyon. From all approaches, at least 25 miles of rough gravel and dirt road await. When dry, the access roads are passable to any vehicle; they are all treacherous when wet. Tight turns and steep grades at the north entrance may be difficult for long trailers. Visitors who have any doubts about road conditions should call the Chaco Canyon Visitor Center (505 786-7014) for the latest information.

Because of its remote location, a trip to Chaco Canyon requires some advance planning. Aside from the campground, no facilities are located in the park. Visitors must fill gas tanks before taking the long dirt roads into the park and bring all the food and other supplies they will need. Food and gasoline can be purchased during the week at the trading posts along NM 44 north of the park.

All trips into the backcountry, including the three described herein, require a free permit available at the Visitor Center. Collecting plants, rocks, or artifacts is prohibited. Also, leave all artifacts where they are found. To prevent damage to the fragile ruins, stay off the walls. Even in the backcountry, stay on the designated trails. All trails close at sunset, so plan hikes accordingly.

The easiest access to Chaco Canyon is from the north via NM 44. From the south, turn onto San Juan County Road 7800 at Nageezi, about 120 miles north of Bernalillo and 32 miles south of Bloomfield. Follow the signs about 12 miles to the junction with NM 57 and turn left. From Bloomfield, take NM 44 south 32 miles to Blanco Trading Post and turn right (south) on the gravel NM 57. From the junction of CR 7800 and NM 57, the Visitor Center is another 11 miles south.

The Alto Mesa Trail is the most popular and diverse backcountry trail at Chaco Canyon. Modern visitors can easily sense the central role that Pueblo Alto played in Anasazi commerce. Perched on the very top of the mesa, Pueblo Alto and its attendant smaller ruins have a view of many places significant in the Anasazi world, such as Mount Taylor and the San Juan Mountains. Roads from towns within the canyon and to outlying sites as far as 40 miles away converge at Pueblo Alto.

The Alto Mesa Loop begins along the park road directly behind Kin Kletso, about 5 miles west of the Visitor Center. From behind Kin Kletso, a sign marks the beginning of the trail. Follow the well-worn, winding path up the talus along the cliff face, using caution. The trail soon enters and climbs a narrow crack in the rocks. Once on the first bench level of the mesa, follow the copious rock cairns as they lead east along the slickrock.

The trail parallels the cliff face, winding around the heads of several canyons. In 0.5 mile from the start, the return leg of the loop enters from the direction of the Pueblo Alto ruins to the left. Take a short cairned route to the right to the overlook of Pueblo Bonito almost directly below. Return to the main route and turn right, continuing along the slickrock bench. Climb a short spur of the mesa, then descend along a cliff that offers views of Chetro Ketl.

The trail skirts the head of another box canyon and then follows a short segment of an ancient road alignment. The road is clear of loose

Pueblo Bonito from the Alto Mesa Trail

rocks and is bordered by a low masonry wall. Round the end of this spur of the mesa and climb steeply to the next bench level. In about 200 yards, climb again through a narrow crack to the top of the ridge. After rounding the upper end of the canyon, a marked viewpoint provides the best perspective on the Jackson Stairs, a precarious ancient route from canyon bottom to mesa top.

After a few minutes heading west on the slickrock, the trail climbs a sandy hill, leading in 0.5 mile to the remains of the Pueblo Alto complex. From the ruin, the view encompasses hundreds of square miles to the north, extending from the La Plata mountains in southern Colorado to Mount Taylor in the south. Line-of-sight connections can be made with ruins to the north, a signal station in South Gap, Tsin Kletzin on the mesa on the opposite site of Chaco Canyon, and Mount Taylor to the south.

From Pueblo Alto, a sign points the way back to the trailhead. Head south for 0.5 mile, turn right onto the trail taken earlier, and then descend the crack to the parking area.

38 SOUTH MESA LOOP

Managed by: Chaco Canyon National Historical Park
Distance: 5 miles, day hike
Elevation range: 6,100 to 6,650 feet
Elevation gain: 550 feet
Difficulty: moderate
Seasons: all year
Water: carry water
Map: Chaco National Historical Park brochure
Interesting features: lightly used trail, scenic overlooks, large unexcavated ruin

South Gap, a wide break in the south wall of Chaco Canyon, and South Mesa played a central role in the Chaco communication system, a complex series of line-of-sight connections between villages. The largest pueblos were probably sited near the South Gap due to the ease of travel through the gap into the canyon. A signal station near the South Gap Overlook on this hike provided a visual link between Pueblo Alto and Pueblo Bonito. Perhaps no other village demonstrates the importance of the line-of-sight concept as well as Tsin Kletzin. Move the location of the town a hundred yards in any direction and visual connections with other Chaco sites are lost.

Driving directions to Chaco Canyon are found in the Alto Mesa Loop (No. 37) hike description. The South Mesa Trail begins at the parking area for Casa Rinconada, about 4 miles west of the Visitor Center on the eastbound side of the main park road. From the parking area, begin by following the Casa Rinconada interpretive trail. In 50 feet, bear right onto a gravel path heading toward Casa Rinconada. On the back side of the ruin, find a post marked "South Mesa Loop." Turn

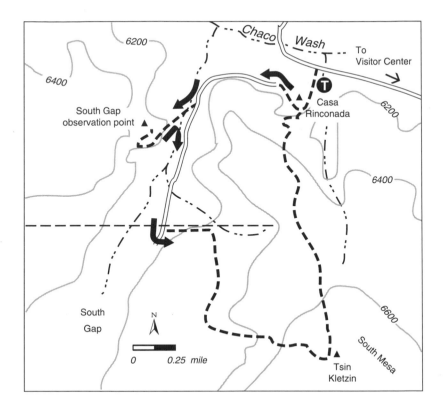

right onto a dirt path that heads west, parallel to the base of the cliff. After 0.1 mile, bear left onto a service road, which leads into South Gap. After passing the end of South Mesa, pass an intersection with a trail from Pueblo del Arroyo to the right.

About 0.75 mile from the start, bear right onto a spur trail heading across the gap to climb to the South Gap observation point. Make the 150-foot climb on a single switchback to the viewpoint. Line-of-sight connections are made with Pueblo Bonito and Pueblo Alto. Do not wander beyond the protective fence.

Backtrack to the service road. Turn right to continue south on the road. In about 0.5 mile, follow the signs for the South Mesa Trail as they lead off the service road and through a fence. The trail immediately turns left to parallel the fence and road, heading east into a broad rincon, a drainage enclosed on three sides by rock walls. In a few minutes, the trail bears right into a long side canyon. At the head of the canyon, bear left and follow a switchback up to the top of a ridge, then climb through white, orange, and tan layers of sandstone toward the top of South Mesa. Watch for cairns and lines of rocks that indicate the location of the trail as it climbs.

Round concretions weathered from sandstone along the South Mesa Trail

From the top of the rocks, the trail climbs the final 0.5 mile to Tsin Kletzin, a ruin about 3.5 miles from the start. Note the line-of-sight connections with Pueblo Alto to the north and the Chaco outlier Kin Klizhin through South Gap.

A post below the northeast corner of Tsin Kletzin marks the 1.5-mile return trail back to Casa Rinconada. Descend across a sandy flat, then drop steeply down layers of sandstone as the trail approaches the cliff. Just above Chaco Canyon are fine views of the major ruins at the foot of the cliff on both sides of the canyon.

39 PEÑASCO BLANCO

Managed by: Chaco Canyon National Historical Park
Distance: 5 miles, day hike
Elevation range: 6,100 to 6,400 feet
Elevation gain: 300
Difficulty: easy
Seasons: all year
Water: carry water
Map: Chaco National Historical Park brochure
Interesting features: large collection of petroglyphs, supernova pictograph, impressive Anasazi ruin, expansive views

Near the ruins of Peñasco Blanco, a short spur trail leads to the most intriguing rock art to be found at Chaco. On a small overhang along the south wall of the canyon, a red-painted crescent moon, large

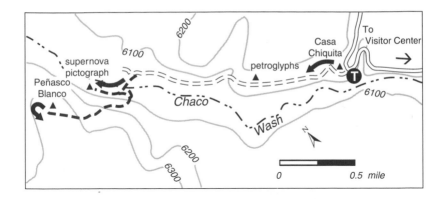

star, and handprint adorn the sandstone. Experts speculate the pictograph represents a supernova explosion that occurred in 1064, during the height of the Anasazi culture in Chaco. Chinese astronomers left a written record of the sudden appearance of a bright new star located near the waxing moon. Ardent skywatchers, the Anasazi certainly witnessed the same event, and this unique rock painting may be their own pictorial record of the explosion.

For driving directions to Chaco Canyon refer to the Alto Mesa Loop (No. 37) hike description. The trailhead to Peñasco Blanco is located along the main park road at Casa Chiquita, about 6 miles west of the Visitor Center. From the trailhead, walk the wide dirt road parallel to Chaco Wash and at the base of the north wall of the canyon. After 0.5 mile of easy walking, look for an arrow pointing to a trail that travels against the very base of the cliff where many petroglyph panels adorn the smooth faces of sandstone. A particularly striking panel—a tapestry design, bighorn sheep, and a human figure—is pecked high on the canyon wall, about 0.75 mile from the start.

After a large panel of rock art, the trail bears left to rejoin the road, which now angles away from the cliff to the center of the canyon. About 1.7 miles from the start, the trail leaves the road on the left and drops into the wash. Immediately come to a trail junction and bear right on the fork signed for "Pictograph." In a minute, the trail crosses the bottom of the wash. *Do not enter the wash when running water is present.* At a trail junction 0.2 mile beyond the wash, bear right. Reach the supernova pictograph in a few minutes. The trail is closed beyond this site.

From the pictograph, backtrack to the last trail junction and continue straight on the fork signed "Ruins." Follow the trail along the cliff face, then climb the ledges to reach the main trail about 0.25 mile from the pictograph. Turn right onto the main trail and follow the many rock cairns as they lead up the ledges to bench level, with Peñasco Blanco in sight most of the way. The ruin lies high atop the mesa, with outstanding views in all directions.

On the return, bypass the side trail to the pictograph by continuing straight at the junction and dropping down the ledges into Chaco

The supernova pictograph along the trail to Pueblo Peñasco

Wash. As the trail swings left, enjoy a walk through the willows for 0.2 mile until the two trails meet near the exit from the wash. Return to the trailhead via the old road.

GOOSEBERRY SPRINGS TRAIL

Managed by: Cibola National Forest, Mt. Taylor Ranger District
Distance: 6 miles, day hike
Elevation range: 9,300 to 11,300 feet
Elevation gain: 2,000 feet
Difficulty: moderate
Seasons: late May through early November
Water: carry water
Maps: Cibola National Forest, USGS Mt. Taylor 7.5' quadrangle
Interesting features: huge, open meadows; outstanding views

Mount Taylor is an extinct volcano rising high above the surrounding lava fields near Grants, New Mexico. The mountain is part of a much larger volcanic field extending to Arizona in the west and to the jagged volcanic necks, tall spires of hardened magma, to the east. The mountain was built by periodic eruptions occurring four to two million years ago. At the end of this period, the peak stood much higher than at present. Subsequent eruptions were of the explosive type and the sideways blasts tore the mountain apart, creating a high-rimmed crater draining to the east.

The Gooseberry Springs Trail climbs to the summit of the rim of the ancient volcano, 5,000 feet above the plains below, creating a commanding view. This is a dry hike, with little or no water available at Gooseberry Springs any time of the year. The exposed meadows near and around the summit make this a risky place to be during the summer thunderstorm season. This trail is best hiked in late May, June, or after mid-September, or early on a summer morning.

From Santa Fe Avenue in Grants, take NM 547 (First Street) north, following the signs for Mount Taylor. Continue about 13 miles to the end of the pavement and turn right onto FR 193. Travel on this well-graded gravel road 5 miles to a small sign on the left marking the beginning of Trail 77. (The junction of FR 193 and FR 501 is 0.1 mile beyond the trailhead.)

The first part of the trail climbs gently through the conifer forest parallel to a small drainage. In 0.25 mile, the trail crosses the drainage to meet an old road and a new section of trail, which is marked as Trail No. 77. Now climb through an airy aspen stand on the right side of the drainage, passing a steel tank at Gooseberry Springs about 0.75 mile from the start.

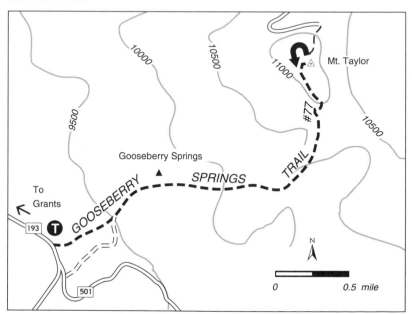

The Goosebury Springs Trail crosses the extensive meadows surrounding Mount Taylor.

At mile 1.1, the trail leaves the forest and enters the extensive meadows surrounding the summit of Mount Taylor. Here the trail follows an old road as it climbs to cross a ridge about 1.5 miles from the start, with long-range views to the south and east. Swing north (left), climbing toward the summit visible straight ahead. The trail crosses the open meadow with a series of broad switchbacks. Just below the summit, pass through a gate, then make the final climb to the top. The horseshoe-shaped rim of the old volcano is clearly visible to the east. After enjoying the view, return to the trailhead by the same route.

41 OSO RIDGE

Managed by: Cibola National Forest, Mt. Taylor Ranger District
Distance: 5 miles, day hike
Elevation range: 8,000 to 8,725 feet
Elevation gain: 725 feet
Difficulty: easy
Seasons: March through November
Water: carry water
Map: USGS Post Office Flat 7.5' quadrangle
Interesting features: seldom-used trail, views of El Malpais

Although an extensive range, the Zuni Mountains have few maintained hiking trails. However, logging and mining roads lace the area. Hikers in the Zunis should try climbing Oso Ridge on FR 50R. Like most of the side roads in the Zunis, this one receives little use by vehicles. The hike is particularly lovely on early summer mornings, exhibiting the interesting mix of bird life found in the Zunis. Among others, expect to find acorn woodpeckers, Williamson's sapsuckers, band-tailed pigeons, pygmy nuthatches, Clark's nutcrackers, and Steller's jays.

Reach the trailhead via NM 53. About 27 miles south of Grants, turn right onto FR 50. Continue on this graded gravel and dirt road about 15 miles to FR 50R, which is about 1 mile south of the junction with FR 480.

From the intersection with FR 50, begin walking west on FR 50R. After a few minutes, take the right fork and enter an open pine forest. As the road swings west, climb a low ridge. All around are signs of logging. Few trees are older than 60 years, and abundant rotting stumps bear testimony to the size of the trees that were harvested many decades ago.

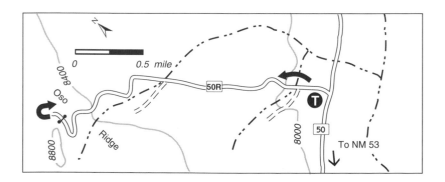

Porcupine prickly pear

About a mile from the start, begin to drop into a grassy valley. The road soon splits; bear right to continue on the main track. Cross the bottom of the valley, then at a minor intersection, the road swings left to parallel the drainage. After an odd stretch of barren rock, the climb steepens, passing through deep ponderosa pine forest.

Two miles from the start, climb through several broad switchbacks, then make the final, rocky climb to the ridge. Pass through a gate, then walk along the road to the left to reach an opening in the trees where, on a clear day, the view north extends to Arizona, 40 miles away. Return by the same route.

 BIG TUBES

Managed by: El Malpais National Monument
Distance: 2 miles, day hike
Elevation range: 7,600 to 7,640 feet
Elevation gain: 50 feet
Difficulty: easy
Seasons: March to December
Water: carry water
Maps: El Malpais Recreation Guide Map, USGS Ice Caves 7.5' quadrangle
Interesting features: lava tubes, lava flow features

The sprawling El Malpais National Monument and Conservation Area is jointly administered by the National Park Service and the Bureau of Land Management. It features some of the most recent lava flows in North America, perhaps as young as 400 years old.

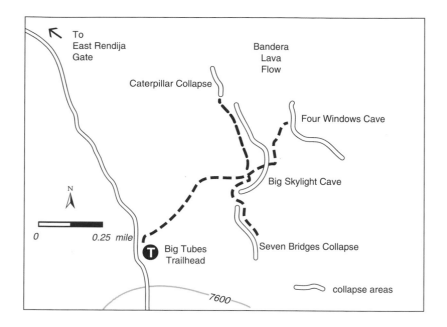

Lava from the most recent eruption of Bandera Crater flowed over 20 miles from the base of the cone almost to Grants. Within the flow is a chain of lava tubes and collapses about 12 miles long. The tubes extending from Bandera Crater exhibit large and small holes in their ceilings: big holes are called skylights, smaller ones, windows. Below the openings, in a cool, wet habitat with plenty of sunlight, a unique community of green moss and insects is found. Help protect these biotic habitats by staying off the mosses. Come prepared to explore underground by bringing three sources of light, such as a lantern, flashlight, and matches and a candle.

Making the trip to the Big Tubes area requires some careful planning and a bit of luck. The main access road into the area, County Road 42, is notoriously impassable when wet, with huge puddles blocking motorized access for weeks after prolonged rains. Make the trip only during dry spells: late May through early July and mid-September to November are best. Under dry conditions, the road is rough but passable to most vehicles, although high clearance is recommended. For the latest road conditions, contact the El Malpais Visitor Center in Grants at (505) 285-5406.

From the west side of Grants, take NM 53 south toward El Malpais and El Morro National Monuments for 26 miles (about 1 mile past the entrance to Bandera Crater and Ice Caves) to County Road 42. Turn left and continue 4.6 miles on this rough road to East Rendija Gate. Turn left and drive 3.2 miles to the Big Tubes Trailhead. Pick up a brochure and cave map at the trailhead.

The rough trail to the Big Tubes is marked with large cairns. From the information board, find the first cairn and walk to it, then sight the next cairn. Continue in this stepwise manner over the Bandera lava flow, watching for the features of recent flows: blocky and jagged aa, the smooth, ropy surface of pahoehoe, and pressure ridges can all be easily examined at close range along the trail.

Slow walking for 0.5 mile leads to the extensive tube and collapse area. Here the main trail ends at a sign that directs hikers to the three trail branches beyond. Explore all three branches. From the sign, the trail left to the entrance to Big Skylight Cave is not apparent. Take a few steps up, staying on the south side of the collapse, to locate the cairned trail. The entrance to Big Skylight is a hundred yards from the sign. The route drops over the wall of the collapse and is not as formidable as it appears from above. However, exploring this tube is made difficult by the huge blocks that have fallen from the ceiling. Beyond the entrance to Big Skylight Cave, the trail continues along the south rim of the collapse to Caterpillar Collapse.

From the sign at the end of the main trail, cairns along the right fork lead to a peek into the big skylight of the cave of the same name, then continue several hundred yards to Seven Bridges Collapse. This long, interesting trench is spanned by a series of natural bridges. The trail leads into the collapse where hikers can follow the trench for a short distance before reaching private property.

Complex flow patterns in a lava boulder

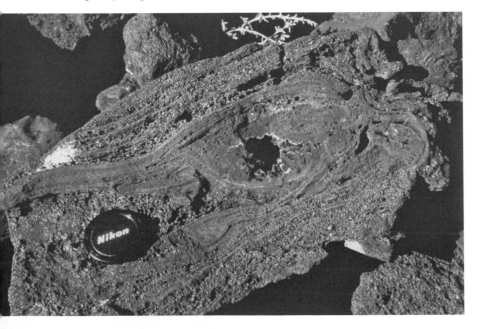

Starting again at the sign at the end of the main trail, the trail branch that begins straight and then veers to the left leads to Four Windows Cave, the most easily explored of the lava tubes in the area. This trail leads along the north rim of a collapse for 200 feet before dropping into a small flat and heading north. Follow the cairns a short 0.25 mile to the rim of another collapse. A cairn on the rim marks an easy route into the trench. Enter the cave, but make certain to stay off the moss-covered rocks. Hikers with the proper equipment can follow the cave its entire 1,200-foot length. Having the detailed Park Service brochure and map will minimize the chance of confusion; it is surprisingly easy to become disoriented in the most remote part of the tube.

43   CERRO AMERICANO

Managed by: Bureau of Land Management, El Malpais National Conservation Area
Distance: 3 miles, day hike
Elevation range: 7,570 to 8,070 feet
Elevation gain: 500
Difficulty: easy
Seasons: March through November
Water: carry water
Maps: El Malpais Recreation Guide Map, USGS Cerro Hueco 7.5' quadrangle
Interesting features: cinder cone, view of volcanic fissure

Cinder cones are huge piles of material spewed from a volcanic vent. Nothing fancy: bits of rock are shot into the air, falling nearby to form a conical mound. Most of the rocks are pebble-sized and called cinders; larger rocks shot higher may cool slightly on the trip down and form volcanic bombs, distinguished by their striated appearance. The resulting piles can rise several hundred feet, forming round hills with small

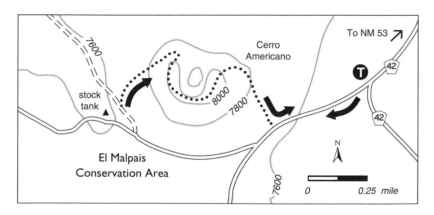

Ponderosa pines, found along the Cerro Americano, have bark that smells like vanilla.

craters in the center. Cerro Americano is one of the highest cinder cones in the Chain of Craters in El Malpais. No trail leads to the summit, but a route that leaves County Road 42 circles to the backside of the cone where climbing to the top is easiest.

From the west side of Grants, take NM 53 south toward El Malpais and El Morro National Monuments for 26 miles (about 1 mile past the entrance to Bandera Crater and Ice Caves) to County Road 42. This road is notoriously impassable when wet, with huge puddles blocking passage for weeks after prolonged rains. Turn left and continue 7.6 miles, past the East, North, and South Rendija gates, to an intersection with a double track road angling to the right. Park off the road.

Begin walking on the double track, heading southwest, with Cerro Americano on the right. The road crosses an open flat, then enters a woodland as it swings by the base of the volcano. At an intersection just short of 0.5 mile from the start, bear right. Views to the left include Cerro Hueco and Cerro Leonides, both along the same rift zone that gave rise to Cerro Americano.

About a mile from the start, just after the road bends gently to the right, take a double track angling to the right. In 200 yards, before the track reaches a small stock tank, leave the track and begin the trailless route around to the north side of Cerro Americano. Bear right and climb through the open woodland on the flank of the volcano. Climb gradually at first, picking up any game or cattle trails that might make walking easier. Work around to the north, enjoying views of the Zuni Mountains to the northwest.

At a grassy meadow on the slopes of the volcano, begin climbing more or less straight up, staying on the west side of a fence that crosses the meadow. Near the rim of the crater, follow the fence to the top. Once on the horseshoe-shaped rim, follow the fence south, then east, then north. From the north side, the views reach beyond the lava flows and cinder cones of El Malpais to Mount Taylor.

From the rim of the crater, visually locate the trailhead below to the east. Get your bearings and drop steeply down the east slope of the volcano, bouncing along through the cinders. At the road, bear left and return to the trailhead.

CENTRAL MOUNTAINS

The Timber Ridge Trail along the grassy crest of the Magdalena Mountains

44 MANZANO PEAK

Managed by: Cibola National Forest, Manzano Wilderness, Mountainair
Ranger District
Distance: 11 miles, day hike or backpack
Elevation range: 8,000 to 10,098 feet
Elevation gain: 2,350 feet
Difficulty: moderate
Seasons: April to November
Water: carry water
Maps: USGS Manzano Peak 7.5' quadrangle, USFS Manzano Wilderness
Interesting features: long-range views, solitude

The Manzano Mountains are a southern extension of the Sandia
Mountains that dominate Albuquerque's skyline. Both ranges have a
similar rugged west face and a sloping eastern flank. The loop hike in
Ox and Kayser canyons is an excellent route to the summit of Manzano
Peak, the highest point of the range. Like most other trails in the
Manzanos, these trails are well-marked and well-maintained, and
walking them is pure pleasure. Views from the crest reach to the isolated mountain ranges beyond the Rio Grande to the west and stretch
for a hundred miles across the plains to the east.

To reach the trailhead, take I 40 east from Albuquerque to exit 175
at Tijeras. Bear right onto NM 337 south, immediately continuing
straight across a T intersection. Travel on NM 337 for 30 miles and
turn right onto NM 55 at a T intersection, then continue 12 miles to
the village of Manzano. Bear right onto NM 131, which is signed for
Manzano Mountains State Park, located 2.5 miles from the village. At
the park entrance, turn right onto FR 253 heading for Red Canyon
Campground. In 2.5 miles, bear left onto FR 422, an all-weather gravel
road. In 2.2 miles, reach a sign for the Ox Canyon Trail No. 190. A
short, rough road to the right leads to a small parking area.

From the trailhead, follow the signs as the Trail No. 190 skirts the
toe of a ridge to enter Ox Canyon, then meets an old route coming up
from the right. The trail turns left, heading up canyon, and at mile 0.2
intersects the Box Spring Canyon Trail No. 99. Bear left to stay in Ox
Canyon and begin a moderate climb through tall Douglas firs. Two
short switchbacks lead past small talus slides made of banded meta-
morphic rock.

As the trail swings left to cross the head of Ox Canyon at mile 1.5,
watch for views down canyon out onto the plains to the east. The trail
now turns in broad switchbacks as it climbs to the crest, meeting the
Crest Trail No. 170 at mile 3.2.

Turn left onto the Crest Trail and continue climbing. The trail soon
turns away from the ridgeline, but continues to climb, gaining the top
of the ridge at mile 3.6. Watch for cairns that mark the trail where it
becomes obscure as it passes through small meadows. At mile 4.5,
intersect the Kayser Trail No. 80. Continue straight on the Crest Trail
heading toward Manzano Peak. Cross a narrow ridge above Kayser

Canyon, then watch for a sign pointing the way to the peak. At the sign, bear away from the main trail to reach the summit at mile 5.2. From the top, views to the west and north include the Manzanos, the Rio Grande valley, and the towns of Belen and Los Lunas.

From the peak, backtrack down to and along the Crest Trail, continuing north toward the Kayser Trail. At the junction with the Kayser Trail, turn right, heading downhill across a meadow to a cairn at the edge of the forest below. From here, the trail is easy to follow through the fir forest as it drops along a ridge and skirts the head of a deep canyon at mile 6.8. Turn widely spaced switchbacks as the trail descends across three drainages, reaching the end of the trail on a four-wheel drive road at mile 8.6.

Turn right and walk down the road, passing the Cottonwood Trail No. 73 at mile 8.9. At mile 9.5, reach FR 422 and turn left. Walk on FR 422 north for 1.5 miles to return to the Ox Canyon Trailhead.

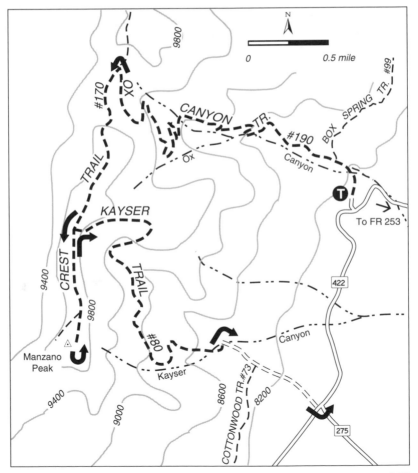

Limestone layers near the crest of the Manzano Mountains (June Fabryka-Martin photo)

45 MANZANO CREST TRAIL

Managed by: Cibola National Forest, Manzano Wilderness, Mountainair Ranger District
Distance: 11.5 miles one-way, day hike or backpack
Elevation range: 7,600 to 9,400 feet
Elevation gain: 1,800 feet
Difficulty: moderate
Seasons: April to November
Water: Upper Fourth of July Spring, carry water
Maps: USGS Capilla Peak and Bosque Peak 7.5' quadrangles, USFS Manzano Wilderness
Interesting features: long hike along mountain crest, views, solitude

One-day loop hikes along the Manzano Crest are difficult to put together, so this long walk along the ridgeline makes setting up the lengthy required shuttle worthwhile. Walking from Capilla Peak north to Fourth of July Campground is a delightful one-way trip that stays on or near the crest of the Manzanos for 9 miles. Views are outstanding for much of the trip, and hikers will likely have the trail to themselves along the little-used middle portions of the route. This hike is especially rewarding in October when the bigtooth maples are blazing red and migrating raptors are commonly sighted following the

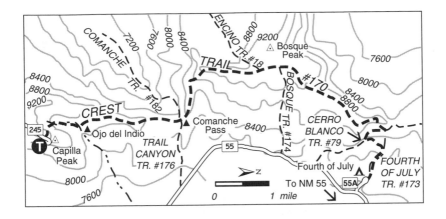

ridgeline. Fossils of ancient sea life are common in the limestone that comprises the crest of the range. Few campsites are found along this route, and water is only found near the end—conditions that require careful planning for an overnight stay.

To set up a shuttle for this hike, from Albuquerque take I 40, NM 337, and NM 55 to Tajique. At the southern end of Tajique, turn right onto FR 55, which is signed for Fourth of July Campground. Go 7 miles to FR 55A and turn right into the campground. Leave a vehicle at the parking area near the campground entrance. Backtrack to Tajique and turn right onto NM 55. Go south about 9 miles to the town of Manzano and turn right onto FR 245, which is signed for Capilla Peak. It is 9 miles to the trailhead near Capilla Peak Campground. The last 4 miles are steep and rough; a high-clearance vehicle is recommended, but low-slung cars frequently make the trip. Park at the sign for the Crest Trail.

Begin hiking downhill on the Crest Trail No. 170, entering a Douglas-fir forest at the head of Cañon del Ojo del Indio. Descend steeply into the canyon on several switchbacks. After passing near the normally dry Ojo del Indio, begin a short climb through shadeless oak scrub. Pass over two low saddles before reaching the top of Comanche Ridge at mile 1.9. There are continual views into Comanche Canyon to the west as the trail passes another saddle and skirts to the west of a knoll before dropping to reach Comanche Pass at mile 3.1.

At a four-way intersection atop Comanche Pass, continue on the Crest Trail past the Comanche Trail No. 182 to the left and the Trail Canyon Trail No. 176 to the right. Begin a long climb by passing through a fenced gate, then bearing left. To the left are views of Capilla Peak and the trail just traveled. At mile 4.1, the trail begins to climb steeply, at first on switchbacks, then cutting across the shoulder of the ridge. As the trail passes a knoll to the west and begins to level, hikers soon gain the ridge and again enjoy views in all directions. Along the crest, watch for abundant fossilized shells in the limestone.

As it approaches the east slope of Bosque Peak, the trail becomes indistinct and hikers must sight from cairn to cairn to stay on the

Looking back to Capilla Peak from the Manzano Crest Trail (June Fabryka-Martin photo)

correct route. The trail passes along the east slope of Bosque Peak to intersect the faint Encino Trail No. 18, and a bit farther on, the Bosque Trail No. 174. Continue north on the Crest Trail across a huge rocky meadow where it is important to follow the cairns marking the trail and not to be misled by cattle trails that criss-cross the area. Begin to descend from Bosque Peak, crossing more meadows and oak scrub along the way. At mile 8.2, reach a saddle that offers views of Albuquerque to the north.

From the saddle, the trail climbs the ridgeline before skirting a low peak to the left. As the trail swings left, Fourth of July Canyon is to the right and the twin Guadalupe and Mosca peaks are straight ahead. Continue dropping to the north, switchbacking down the east side of a ridge at mile 9.2. At mile 9.4, leave the Crest Trail and turn right onto Cerro Blanco Trail No. 79. Begin a long, moderate descent through a shady maple and oak forest on the slopes of Fourth of July Canyon. At mile 10, turn left onto the Fourth of July Trail No. 173 and round the head of several small drainages before reaching the bottom of Fourth of July Canyon. Pass the intersection with the Albuquerque Trail No. 78 at mile 10.5, then drop past Upper Fourth of July Spring. Continue another mile through the shady maples to reach the trailhead at Fourth of July Campground.

46 FOURTH OF JULY/ ALBUQUERQUE LOOP

Managed by: Cibola National Forest, Mountainair Ranger District
Distance: 5 miles, day hike
Elevation range: 7,500 to 8,200 feet
Elevation gain: 800 feet
Difficulty: easy
Seasons: best in fall
Water: Upper Fourth of July Spring, carry water
Maps: USGS Bosque Peak and Tajique 7.5' quadrangles
Interesting features: spectacular fall colors

The short loop through Fourth of July Canyon and Cañon de la Gallina is a New Mexico classic. The dominance of bigtooth maple and Gambel oak in these drainages creates brilliant fall colors that are found in few other locations in the state. The bright red maples outdo the better-known aspen for adding a splash of color to the mountains. Beneath a canopy of fire, this easy autumn stroll is not to be missed. The colors reach their peak in late September and early October.

To reach the trailhead from I 40 at Tijeras, take NM 337 and NM 55 about 35 miles to Tajique. At the southern end of Tajique, turn right

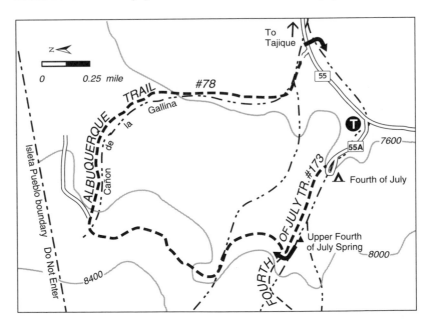

onto FR 55, which is signed for Fourth of July Campground. Go 7 miles to FR 55A, which is past the trailhead for the Albuquerque Trail No. 78, and turn right into the campground. Day parking is available near the campground entrance.

The trailhead is located 0.25 mile up the campground road from the parking area. Begin hiking on the Fourth of July Trail No. 173 as it follows an old road up the canyon bottom. Pass through two gates as the trail climbs on gentle grades. About 0.75 mile from the start, climb more steeply through a rocky, narrow stretch of canyon, passing Upper Fourth of July Spring. Seep spring monkey flowers and horsetails grow in profusion, but keep a watchful eye open for poison ivy, which is common in this canyon. Just past the spring, meet the Albuquerque Trail No. 78. Turn a sharp right onto this trail and begin a steeper climb around a hill and into another small drainage.

At mile 1.2, leave the drainage bottom and climb a dry drainage to a small saddle. Drop into the head of Cañon de la Gallina, for now enjoying the maples from a distance. The trail descends to the canyon bottom and into a fine stand of maples. At mile 3.1, pass a small spring, and soon the trail widens to an old road. At mile 3.7, reach the trailhead for the Albuquerque Trail. Continue to FR 55, turn right and follow the road uphill 0.5 mile to FR 55A. Turn right to return to the trailhead.

Fossil gastropod from the limestones of the Manzano Mountains

47 MAGDELENA CREST TRAIL TO NORTH BALDY

Managed by: Cibola National Forest, Magdalena Ranger District
Distance: 11 miles, day hike
Elevation range: 9,300 to 10,400 feet
Elevation gain: 1,800 feet
Difficulty: strenuous
Seasons: mid-spring to late fall
Water: carry water
Maps: USGS Magdalena and South Baldy 7.5' quadrangles
Interesting features: unparalleled views

The Magdalena Mountains are a small jewel of a mountain range rising out of the deserts of central New Mexico. Their highest point, South Baldy, rises to 10,783 feet. The steep mountain face and grassy summits make possible dramatic views in all directions. The best way to take in the sights is to walk the Magdalena Crest Trail from South Baldy to its lesser neighboring peak, North Baldy. The view along the entire trail takes the eye from the Jemez Mountains far to the north to the Caballo Range in the south, an incredible panorama that encompasses about a tenth of the total land area of New Mexico.

Just south of the summit is the Langmuir Lightning Observatory, located on the crest because of the frequency of summer thunderstorms in the Magdalenas. The crest is no place to be during a thunderstorm, and they are common from late June through early September. Hike the Crest Trail any time of day from April to June. In summer, start early and be off the ridge by noon, sooner if a storm threatens.

To reach the trailhead from Socorro, take US 60 west. Drive about 16 miles to FR 235, marked with a large sign for Water Canyon

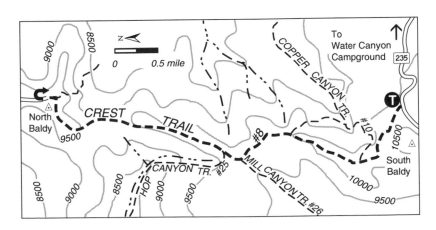

Steep, grassy slopes along the crest of the Magdalena Mountains

Campground, and turn left. Reach the campground and the end of the paved part of the road in 5 miles. Continue on gravel FR 235, which is rough but passable in dry weather to any vehicle, as it climbs into the mountains. The Crest Trailhead is just east of the end of the road, about 8 miles from the campground.

The Crest Trail No. 8 starts on a saddle just east of South Baldy, on the right-hand side of the road. Begin by climbing steeply along a trail up a spur ridge of South Baldy, angling to the left from the parking area. (Do not take the more prominent double-track straight ahead.) At the ridgeline, drop into the deep forest on the other side. Descend several switchbacks before climbing to the main crest, which is reached 0.5 mile from the start. Cross the crest in a grassy meadow, then drop on a short switchback to the west side of the ridge. The trail now swings north to parallel the crest.

At mile 0.8, burst out into a broad meadow with striking views of the San Mateo Mountains to the west. Pass the junction with the Copper Canyon Trail No. 10 to the right. Continue north, climbing to the ridge, then dropping on the west side and crossing two talus slopes. Reach the crest again at mile 1.5, with views east into Copper Canyon, the eastern Magdalenas, and the Rio Grande valley beyond.

As the trail drops to the next saddle, a mining road comes up from the drainage to the left. Climb a few feet to the ridgeline, then drop onto the east side of the crest, watching for rock cairns to mark the way. The trail continues on the east slope, crossing several spur ridges along the way. At mile 2.5, reach another grassy saddle and the Mill Canyon Trail No. 26 coming in from the west. Just as you reenter the woods, reach the junction with the Hop Canyon Trail No. 25. Bear right, staying on the crest. The trail soon becomes a bit more rough and rocky. Climb for 0.25 mile, then make a long descent to a saddle just below North Baldy.

The final 500-foot climb to the summit is through cliffs of white rhyolite. Stay on the trail as it swings around the summit and climb the last few yards to the top from the northeast slope. The 360-degree view from the top makes the ascent worthwhile. Each direction presents a series of overlapping mountain ranges slowly fading with distance. After taking in the sights, return by the same route.

48 COPPER CANYON/ SOUTH BALDY LOOP

Managed by: Cibola National Forest, Magdalena Ranger District
Distance: 11 miles, day hike or backpack
Elevation range: 6,800 to 10,400
Elevation gain: 3,600 feet
Difficulty: strenuous
Seasons: mid-spring to late fall
Water: unreliable in Copper and Water canyons, carry water
Maps: USGS Magdalena and South Baldy 7.5' quadrangles
Interesting features: remote canyons, ridge-top views

This long, challenging loop leads into the heart of the Magdalena Range, climbing the steep mountain face to the crest through one canyon and descending along another. The ascent up Copper Canyon is gentle at first, but steepens as it approaches the ridgeline; Water Canyon provides a gradual drop from the high country. Campsites and water are plentiful along the middle stretch of Copper Canyon but are limited in Water Canyon.

This loop begins and ends at Water Canyon Campground. From Socorro, take US 60 west. Drive about 16 miles to FR 235, marked with a large sign for Water Canyon Campground, and turn left. Reach the campground and the end of the pavement in 5 miles. No water is available.

From the campground, walk back toward the paved road 100 yards to the junction of FR 235 and FR 406. Turn left, then immediately turn right to continue on FR 406. Walk this dirt road, crossing Copper Canyon at mile 0.9. Beyond the crossing near a parcel of private land, a

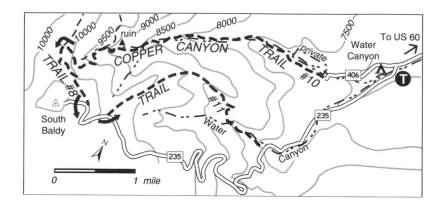

sign points the way to the Copper Canyon Trail No. 10. Begin walking uphill on an old road paralleling a fence bordering private property. The trail skirts a large meadow, passing the ranch house. As the canyon narrows about 1.5 miles from the start, pass a fork in the road angling sharply to the right. Soon the old road narrows to a trail, and the canyon is shaded by large pines. From this point, water is intermittently found in the canyon bottom.

After crossing the stream, the trail gently climbs to the slopes above the canyon bottom. Nice camping spots are plentiful along the stream. At mile 3.8, pass the ruins of a prospector's cabin. Water can be found in the stream near the cabin throughout the year. Just up the canyon, come to the junction of two branches of the trail leading to the crest. Take the left fork, which may be signed for Crest Trail No. 8 and FR 235.

The last mile to the crest is considerably steeper than the trail below. As the switchbacks grow tighter near the ridgeline, enjoy sweeping views down canyon. Reach a meadow just below the crest and follow the faint trail over the top to the junction with the Crest Trail No. 8 at mile 4.8.

Turn left (south) onto Trail No. 8, crossing a grassy slope before reentering the woods. At the next small meadow, the trail turns a switchback over the ridge and descends into the deep forest on the east side. After a brief descent, the trail climbs again to reach a spur ridge just below the summit of South Baldy at mile 5.8. Drop to FR 235, turn left, and begin a 0.5-mile stretch on the road to meet Trail No. 11. At a sign on a broad saddle, turn left onto Trail No. 11 and begin the long descent back to the trailhead.

At the bottom of the first steep pitch is a lovely pine-covered saddle that makes a good waterless campsite. Beyond the saddle, the trail drops steadily along a long spur ridge, with views through the trees back to the grassy slopes of the crest. After crossing the ridge, the trail winds through several drainages. The southern exposure creates an extraordinary juxtaposition of plants: on a 20-foot stretch of trail, hikers can pass yucca, scrub oak, white fir, and alligator juniper.

The San Mateo Mountains as seen from the Magdalena Crest Trail

At mile 8.5, the trail switchbacks down to the bottom of Water Canyon. The trail is now less steep as it follows the canyon floor. A reliable water flow is reached at mile 8.8 and a few shady campsites can be found downstream. Reach FR 235 at mile 9.3. Turn left onto the road and continue down Water Canyon another 2 miles to the campground and trailhead.

49 TIMBER PEAK TRAIL

Managed by: Cibola National Forest, Magdalena Ranger District
Distance: 6 miles, day hike
Elevation range: 9,800 to 10,300 feet
Elevation gain: 1,200 feet
Difficulty: moderate
Seasons: mid-spring to early winter
Water: carry water
Map: USGS South Baldy 7.5' quadrangle
Interesting features: long-distance views, wild ridge and canyon scenery, solitude

In a mountain range known for its sweeping views, the Timber Peak Trail offers the most dramatic panoramas. In addition to endless horizons, this trail includes striking views of deep canyons within the range. The attractive scenery along Timber Ridge makes even a short hike along it rewarding.

Avoid this trail on summer afternoons when thunderstorms are likely. Beyond 1.5 miles, this trail can be difficult to follow and hikers should be comfortable following an occasionally obscure trail marked with rock cairns and tree blazes.

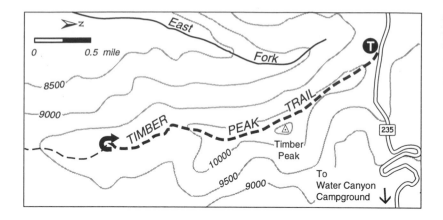

From Socorro, take US 60 west. Drive about 16 miles to FR 235, marked with a large sign for Water Canyon Campground, and turn left. Reach the campground and the end of the paved part of the road in 5 miles. Continue on gravel FR 235 as it climbs into the mountains. The Timber Peak Trail is 6.7 miles from the end of the pavement, and the trailhead is well-marked on the left (south) side of the road. FR 235 is rough and steep but passable in dry weather to any vehicle.

From the trailhead sign, climb steeply on the grassy ridgeline to the southeast, with rock cairns marking the way. In several hundred yards, the trail crosses a dip in the crest and becomes easy to follow on the west flank of the ridge. The view extends as far as Elephant Butte Reservoir to the south. Soon the trail rises to the ridgeline and again follows the crest, with Timber Peak straight ahead. At times the trail is faint and hikers should watch for double blazes on the trees. Reach the foot of Timber Peak at mile 0.8, then enter a fir-spruce-limber pine forest.

The trail contours west of Timber Peak, scratched into a steep slope. After crossing a talus field, the trail climbs steeply to the ridge and follows the crest on its east side. The trail dips and climbs along the ridge, passing through an open aspen stand. Along the ridge, note (and take warning from) the abundance of lightning-scarred trees.

At mile 2, the ridge takes a jog to the east. Here the trail turns left and descends to a broad saddle. Carefully locate the trail marked with cairns and blazes as it heads east across the saddle. As the trail becomes easier to follow, it climbs steeply up the hill on the other side. Again the trail is on the east side of the ridgeline. Follow the cairns across an open meadow, descending gradually to reenter the trees. Enter another broad meadow at mile 2.8 and angle toward the ridgeline to enjoy the views to the west.

The meadow makes a good turnaround point. The trail continues another 2 miles along the ridge to a helispot below the summit of Italian Peak. Beyond the turnaround, the trail is difficult to follow and fails to offer the constant, dramatic views of the first section.

Old blazes mark the Timber Ridge Trail.

50 POTATO CANYON

Managed by: Cibola National Forest, Withington Wilderness, Magdalena
    Ranger District
Distance: 6 miles one-way, day hike
Elevation range: 6,800 to 9,800 feet
Elevation gain: 3,000-foot descent
Difficulty: moderate
Seasons: April to November
Water: intermittent flow in Potato Canyon
Maps: USGS Mount Withington 7.5' quadrangle, USFS Apache Kid and
    Withington Wildernesses
Interesting features: isolated mountain range, wild country, scenic waterfall

The northern half of the long San Mateo Mountains holds one of
New Mexico's least-used wilderness areas, the Withington. Because
this wilderness area is so far from the normal tourist routes, just driving to it can be an adventure. This range is for experienced hikers who

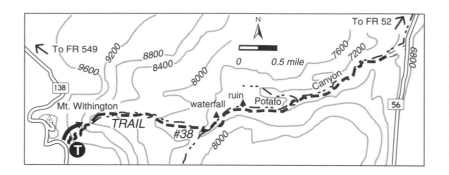

can follow ill-defined trails. Help is far away, so prepare carefully for any trip to the area. A topographic map and compass will help with route finding on the little-used and difficult-to-follow upper section of this trail.

Potato Canyon, named for a rounded rock spire on a bordering ridge, holds the most accessible trail in the range. Dropping from the crest of the range near 10,000 feet, the canyon traverses all the dominant southwestern life zones from alpine forest to juniper woodlands. The walk on the brittle shales of the lower canyon is pleasantly shaded by a canopy of Arizona walnut. Because the trail is easier to follow starting from the western trailhead, this trip is described as a one-way descent from summit to valley.

To set up a shuttle from Magdalena, take NM 107 south. This dirt road is passable to all vehicles when dry. Go about 17 miles to the intersection with FR 52 and bear right. Take this rough road for 3.5 miles to FR 56 and bear left. A high-clearance vehicle will make the 3-mile journey to the trailhead a bit easier. After leaving a vehicle, return to FR 52 and turn left. In 11 rough miles, turn left on FR 549, a good dirt road. Turn left and continue 8.5 miles to FR 138. Turn left and drive about 4 miles past the Mount Withington Lookout to the trailhead. If the long drive is unappealing, even an in-and-out hike from FR 52 into the bottom of Potato Canyon makes it worthwhile.

Trail No. 38 starts on a narrow saddle just south of the summit of Mount Withington. Begin hiking downhill through the conifer forest along the crest. The trail is often very faint; hikers must watch carefully to stay on the route and make certain they do not stray from it. Frequent switchbacks cut the trail steeply down from the crest, crossing the bottom of a small canyon several times on the way. At mile 1.6, the trail reaches the bottom of a larger canyon. Bear left and follow the trail down the canyon bottom. The trail is well-marked with blazes, but hikers must watch for them carefully. The route parallels the canyon bottom from here to the lower trailhead; if the trail is lost, simply follow the stream bed.

In this first stretch of the canyon, the trail wanders from stream bed to the forest just above the stream. Large boulders in the canyon bottom make it easier to follow the trail in this stretch. At mile 3.4, intersect the main branch of Potato Canyon entering from the right. Several nice campsites are located on the benches above the stream in this area. Just down the canyon, the trail turns right to climb high above the canyon floor to skirt around a narrows, but continue straight ahead in the canyon bottom. At mile 3.7, reach a lovely spot with a small waterfall.

The trail rejoins the canyon bottom route at mile 4. Continue on the trail, passing on the left the ruins of a cabin at mile 4.4. The canyon begins to open up as the trail passes beneath soaring cliffs of pink rock. Pass a major side canyon entering from the left at mile 5.2 and continue on either the trail or the stream bed to the wilderness boundary at mile 6.7. Here the trail widens to a road, reaching the parking area in 0.4 mile.

Small waterfall in Potato Canyon (Bob Julyan photo)

VICKS PEAK

Managed by: Cibola National Forest, Apache Kid Wilderness, Magdalena
  Ranger District
Distance: 12 miles, backpack
Elevation range: 7,400 to 10,250 feet
Elevation gain: 3,100 feet
Difficulty: strenuous
Seasons: April to November
Water: Nave Spring, San Mateo Spring
Maps: USGS Vicks Peak and Blue Mountain 7.5' quadrangles, USFS
  Withington and Apache Kid Wildernesses
Interesting features: wild country, great views, solitude

The Apache Kid Wilderness is located in the southern half of the
San Mateo Mountains. Named for a renegade Apache reportedly buried there, the wilderness has almost 100 miles of primitive trails, but
very few access points. The lower half of the wilderness is easily
reached from Springtime Campground, and hikers with ample time
can take trips of over 50 miles into the central range. The Apache Kid
Wilderness can get hot in summer, but the usually light snowfalls in
the range make it an ideal spot for a spring or late fall trip.

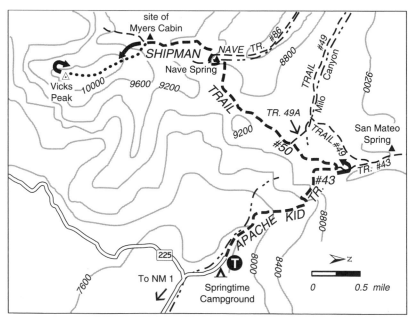

Tarantulas look dangerous but are harmless.

The journey to the summit of Vicks Peak is an excellent introduction to the range. It is a long and strenuous hike to the summit, too much for most hikers to make in one day. Start with plenty of water, and plan to replenish the supply at San Mateo and Nave Springs. Waterless campsites are located on the flat saddle at the site of Myers Cabin near the base of Vicks Peak. Plan to reach Myers Cabin the first day, then visit the peak the next morning before returning to the trailhead.

To reach Springtime Campground from Socorro, leave I 25 at exit 115, which is about 45 miles south of town. Get on NM 1 and continue south, parallel to the interstate about 10 miles to FR 225. Turn right and follow FR 225 13.5 miles to the entrance to Springtime Campground. Turn right, enter the campground, and park at the trailhead for Trail No. 43.

Begin hiking on the well-maintained Apache Kid Trail No. 43. Under ponderosa pines, the first section of trail makes a moderate climb that can be hot from late spring through the summer. The trail ascends a small drainage for 1.2 miles before bearing west and beginning a steep climb on switchbacks. At mile 2.1, reach an intersection on a saddle at the foot of a rocky knob. With the most difficult portions of the hike behind, take a long rest before turning left onto the Shipman Trail No. 50. (Water is found at San Mateo Spring, 0.5 mile north on Trail No. 43.) Trail No. 50 is not as easy to follow as Trail No. 43, but numerous markers help keep hikers on the correct route.

Trail No. 50 stays atop a broad ridge before dropping into the head of Milo Canyon, reaching the bottom at mile 2.7. Pass the junction with Trail No. 49A, a branch of the Milo Trail No. 49, to the right. Continue straight, switchbacking up to another saddle at mile 3.3. Traversing conifer forest, the trail again drops, this time to reach Nave Spring at mile 4.3, where a small but dependable flow of water is located just down from the trail. After the spring, climb steeply to the intersection with the Nave Trail No. 86, then cross another saddle. Again drop into a small drainage before climbing to a broad saddle at mile 5.2. This is the site of Myers Cabin, and campsites are easily located in the open forest.

From the saddle, a faint, unmaintained path climbs the ridge to the southeast. Leave Trail No. 50 and angle up through the forest by the easiest route. At mile 5.7, the forest opens up near the base of an unnamed peak. Continue over the peak, then follow the ridge to the southeast to the wooded summit of Vicks Peak. The spectacular view from the peak reaches far east to the Capitan Range and south to the Elephant Butte and Caballo reservoirs along the Rio Grande. Return by the same route.

52 BROAD CANYON

Managed by: Bureau of Land Management, Las Cruces District
Distance: 4 miles, day hike
Elevation range: 4,750 to 5,100 feet
Elevation gain: 650 feet
Difficulty: easy
Seasons: September to May
Water: carry water
Maps: USGS Sierra Alta and Souse Springs 7.5' quadrangles
Interesting features: Chihuahuan Desert vegetation, narrow canyons, petroglyphs

The foothills at Broad Canyon are softly stroked with creosote bush and the rolling slopes are slashed with cliffs of tan volcanic rocks tilted this way and that. For those who enjoy something a bit different, it is a place of solitude and wild exploring. Both Valles and Broad canyons are narrow defiles filled with rocky delights: swirling water-cut channels carved into the soft tuff, huge rounded boulders tumbled by flash floods, and tight, unexpected bends in the canyon floors. Much of this hike passes through private land on an easement and hikers should stay on the described route.

Travel north on I 25 from Las Cruces about 15 miles to NM 157. Exit and go west for 2 miles to NM 185. Turn right and go another 12 miles, then turn left onto the easy-to-miss County Road E006. This road has a few rough spots but when dry is passable to all vehicles. In 7.5 miles, near the Cothran Ranch water tanks, bear left at a fork, passing through a gate. In 0.2 mile, come to another fork. This time take the right fork and park in another 0.1 mile just before the road pitches down the canyon wall.

Begin walking down the shelf road into Broad Canyon, which at this point is indeed a wide gash through the grassland hills. The road continues along the canyon bottom. At mile 1.4, the road turns away from the canyon and climbs over a low saddle, passing a stock tank halfway up. Over the saddle, descend to again meet Broad Canyon. Now turn left, leaving the road, and follow the slickrock of the canyon bottom. This is the meat of the hike, walking on scoured tuff in the deepening canyon. Boulder-hop down canyon about 0.5 mile to where Valles Canyon enters from the right. Watch for petroglyphs on the walls before exploring up Valles Canyon, a twisting, narrow watercourse full of surprises. Be alert for rattlesnakes sunning themselves on the rocks, particularly in spring.

Backtrack down to Broad Canyon, turning right to continue down it for a few hundred yards past a soaring wall of red tuff to a fence that marks private property. Hikers must turn around here, but they can pause to enjoy the shade of a cluster of large oaks before returning to the road by backtracking upstream. Once at the road, turn right and return to the car park by the same route.

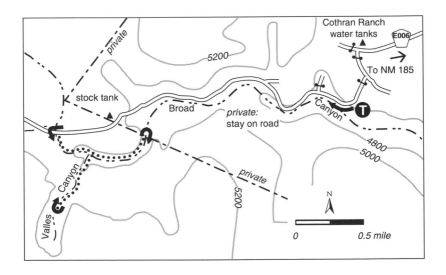

53 INDIAN HOLLOW

Managed by: Bureau of Land Management, Aguirre Springs Recreation
Area, Las Cruces District
Distance: 5 miles, day hike or backpack
Elevation range: 5,200 to 6,800 feet
Elevation gain: 1,500 feet
Difficulty: strenuous
Seasons: all year
Water: at the campground, intermittent flow in Indian Hollow
Maps: USGS Organ and Organ Peak 7.5' quadrangles
Interesting features: sheer granite cliffs, large alligator junipers, secluded
canyon

The granite crags of the Organ Mountains are one of the most spectacular features of southern New Mexico. The east face of the range
jumps abruptly from the desert floor near Las Cruces, and the ragged
towers of vertically jointed granite are said to resemble the tubes of a
pipe organ. Much of the Organs are under the jurisdiction of the White
Sands Missile Range and are off limits to visitors. The best access to
the range is at the Aguirre Springs Recreation Area and the primitive
route into Indian Hollow is the most interesting hike. Although Indian
Hollow is near the developed campground, it is rugged country with
confusing terrain. Few visitors make the trek into the canyon.

To reach the trailhead from the junction of I 25 and US 70 in Las

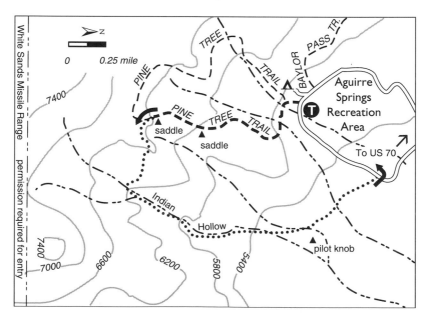

Alligator juniper bark

Cruces, go east on US 70 toward San Augustin Pass. About 14 miles from the interstate, turn right onto the road to Aguirre Springs Recreation Area. Continue about 6 miles to the Pine Tree trailhead and park. Note that a small fee is charged for day use in the recreation area.

Begin climbing on the Pine Tree Trail in a huge amphitheater of granite, with towering cliffs in three directions. This north-facing slope supports a surprisingly lush plant community dominated by huge alligator junipers. At 0.25 mile from the start, the Pine Tree Trail splits into two branches. Take the left fork and continue climbing, with views of Baylor Pass to the right. Just short of mile 1, reach a saddle and cross over to the opposite side of the ridge with views of conical Sugarloaf Peak straight ahead. Continue climbing to a second saddle at mile 1.5 where a short spur left leads to a viewpoint.

Within 200 feet of the saddle, a second, fainter trail angles off to the left. Take this lesser-used trail, which leads to Indian Hollow. Follow the light tread south, watching for rock cairns that mark the way. Continue climbing, steeply at times, skirting around the head of a side canyon. After about 0.5 mile on this faint trail, reach a spur ridge with steep canyons on either side. Drop off the east face of the ridge and descend into Indian Hollow, carefully picking a route down to the canyon bottom. Use caution on the steep slope. A trickle of water is usually found in this section of Indian Hollow, and shady and level ground make it an interesting place for an overnight stay. Hikers can explore up two canyons heading south, but be on the watch for the boundary of the White Sands Missile Range about 0.5 mile away—do not enter without permission.

To return to the trailhead, walk down Indian Hollow. Trails come and go along the way, but the stream bed is easy to follow. After 1.25 miles, watch closely for rock cairns that mark a trail to the left that leads to the main road. The trail crosses several drainages before crossing a low saddle just to the south of a distinctive knob on the ridge. The trail here is faint; head generally west to reach the main road. At the road, turn left and walk uphill to return to the parking area in about 0.75 mile.

54   BAYLOR PASS

Managed by: Bureau of Land Management, Aguirre Springs Recreation Area, Las Cruces District
Distance: 6 miles one-way, day hike
Elevation range: 4,900 to 6,380 feet
Elevation gain: 750 feet
Difficulty: easy
Seasons: all year
Water: at the main campground only, carry water
Maps: USGS Organ Peak and Organ 7.5' quadrangles
Interesting features: historic pass, scenic views, easy shuttle

The National Recreation Trail over Baylor Pass roughly follows the route taken by the Confederate cavalry hile engaging the Union infantry in 1862 during the Civil War. Near Las Cruces, Colonel John Baylor was attacked by Union troops under Major Isaac Lynde. Baylor's inferior force nonetheless held its ground against the Union, and apparently the sight of blood was enough to send Lynde packing out of nearby Fort Fillmore, a supply base he considered indefensible. Legend has it that, as the Union soldiers destroyed the supplies at Fort Fillmore in preparation for their retreat, they were loath to pour out a store of good medicinal whisky, instead using it to fill their canteens. As they

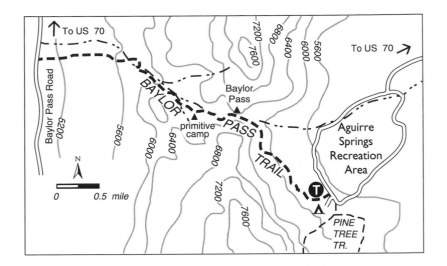

retreated toward San Augustin Pass, the July sun and whisky soon dehydrated the marchers. Baylor easily caught Lynde's stragglers, who readily surrendered for a drink of water. Then Baylor and several hundred mounted troops dashed across the pass that would bear his name, and surprised Lynde's main Union force at San Augustin Spring, where Lynde accepted Baylor's demand for unconditional surrender.

This hike is best done with a shuttle. Drive east on US 70 from the intersection with I 25 in Las Cruces. In about 11 miles, turn right onto Baylor Pass Road. In 0.8 mile, continue straight over a cattle guard onto a gravel road. A mile beyond, leave a vehicle at the well-marked trailhead on the left side of the road. Return to US 70, turn right, and continue 2 miles over San Augustin Pass to the road to Aguirre Springs Recreation Area. Turn right and continue about 6 miles to the Baylor Pass Trailhead.

Most of the elevation gain to the pass is accomplished in the first mile as the trail winds through juniper-pine woodland. In about a mile, pass directly beneath the lofty Rabbit Ears, twin peaks of craggy granite. Cross over a spur ridge to parallel a drainage leading to Baylor Pass. In spring, hikers will be jolted by a stiff head-wind at this point. Reach the pass about 2 miles from the start and enjoy the long-distance views to the east of Las Cruces, jagged volcanic peaks, and the Black Range on the far horizon.

From Baylor Pass, the trail switchbacks down through scrub oak, white-thorn acacia, and manzanita, a striking contrast to the plants on the east side of the mountain. In the round bowl of upper Baylor Canyon, the trail is cut on decomposed granite, which makes for slippery footing. Well into the bowl at 3.3 miles, pass a waterless primitive campground shaded by a single tree.

Organ Mountains from the foot of Baylor Pass

The trail heads toward the mouth of the canyon. Just before arriving there, at a point where a short spur trail leads left to a viewpoint, the trail abruptly turns right and descends. Drop quickly over several switchbacks before crossing the canyon bottom and reaching the alluvial fan. On the open desert, drop through the last mile to the western trailhead.

SOUTHEASTERN MOUNTAINS

Open ponderosa pine forest along the Three Rivers Trail

55 ALKALI FLAT TRAIL

Managed by: White Sands National Monument
Distance: 5 miles, day hike
Elevation range: 3,900 to 4,000 feet
Elevation gain: 100 feet
Difficulty: modeate
Seasons: all year, but best October through April
Water: carry water
Map: USGS Heart of the Sands 7.5' quadrangle
Interesting features: world's largest gypsum dune field, endless exploring, animal tracks

A hike at White Sands is a unique experience. This huge sand pile is composed of gypsum, not the more common quartz. Gypsum sand is soft-grained and smooth, giving these dunes a different, pleasant feel to bare feet. The fine sand also makes for easy animal tracking. The gypsum weathers out of the ancient seabed rocks of the surrounding mountains. It is dissolved and transported by runoff, accumulating in Lake Lucero in the western part of the monument. The gypsum precipitates out of the evaporating lake water and is deposited on the lake bottom. In the desert environment, the lake is most often completely dry. Strong westerly winds then push the gypsum east to pile into large dunes.

Hiking on white sand requires some special preparation. To prevent burning by the sun and its intense reflection off the sand, always use a heavy coat of sunscreen. Dark glasses are also essential to prevent damage to the eye and simply to make the journey more pleasant. No water is available in the dunes, so take an adequate supply. All-terrain sandals or running shoes are the best footwear for dune hiking.

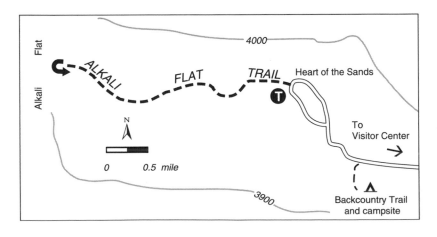

Yucca growing in an interdune basin at White Sands National Monument

Three trails are maintained by the park, but hiking is possible just about anywhere in the dune field. Hikers should pick a location that strikes their fancy or follow the Alkali Flat Trail as described. Note that hikers on this trail are required to register at the trailhead and in all cases to return by sunset. Before setting out cross-country, stop and orient yourself with respect to the San Andres Mountains to the west and the lofty Sacramento Mountains, as well as low-flying jets from Holloman Air Force Base, to the east. These are useful features by which to navigate. Use these landmarks as bearings out on the dunes. If the wind is calm, hikers can easily follow their tracks back to the road.

Camping is permitted only at the lightly used backcountry site at the end of the 0.3 mile Backcountry Trail. A free permit is required for an overnight trip and is available at the Visitor Center. Note that testing at the adjacent White Sands Missile Range occasionally requires the park to close the backcountry to camping.

To reach the trailhead from Alamogordo, take US 54/70 south from town and continue west on US 70 when US 54 bears left. The entrance to White Sands National Monument is about 15 miles southwest of town. Continue about 6 miles on the park road to the Heart of the Sands and the well-marked trailhead.

Begin hiking west on the Alkali Flat Trail. The trail is marked with numerous orange and white posts. Find the first post, then spot the next trail marker before moving on. Continue in this manner, walking from post to post, through the dune field. The trail traverses the dunes themselves and often crosses vegetated interdunal basins. For much of the trip, the San Andres Mountains lie straight ahead. Walking is slow in the soft sand, and distances are difficult to judge. At mile 2.1, the trail reaches the edge of Alkali Flat, the lake bed where gypsum sand is formed. The trail continues out a short distance onto the flats, which can be an unpleasant place when the wind blows. From the flats, return to the trailhead by the same route.

56   DOG CANYON

Managed by: Oliver Lee Memorial State Park, Lincoln National Forest, Cloudcroft Ranger District
Distance: 9 miles, day hike or backpack
Elevation range: 4,400 to 7,500 feet
Elevation gain: 3,300 feet
Difficulty: strenuous
Seasons: September to May
Water: at the Visitor Center and in Dog Canyon at mile 2.5
Maps: USGS Alamogordo South and Sacramento Peak 7.5' quadrangles
Interesting features: historic route, running water, spectacular scenery

Holding permanent running water and a steep route over the rampart of the southern Sacramento Mountains, Dog Canyon has been tramped by Mescalero Apaches, Mexican and American soldiers, and Texas ranchers. It is said that this route to the high country was a particular favorite of Apache war parties because of the ease with which they could ambush pursuers at the "eyebrow" section, which is perched on a narrow ledge below 800-foot walls of limestone. In 1880, the Ninth Cavalry lost several men on the eyebrow when Apaches rolled large boulders down on them from above.

The Dog Canyon Trail follows the historic route from the Tularosa Valley to Joplin Ridge. It is a steep, arduous climb with no shade or water for the first 2.5 miles: avoid Dog Canyon in mid-summer. The

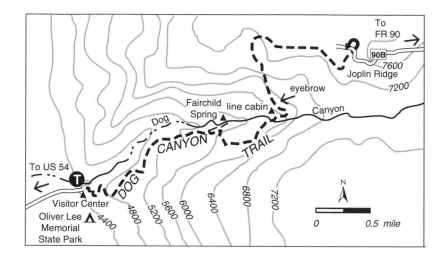

scenery is grand every step of the way, displaying the harsh beauty of the Chihuahuan Desert. Limestone cliffs deposited on the ocean floor about 250 million years ago soar over 3,000 feet above. Below is the Tularosa Valley, a huge fault-block basin with no outlet.

To reach the trailhead from Alamogordo, take US 54 south from US 70 in the south part of town. Drive 8 miles to Dog Canyon Road, which is signed for Oliver Lee Memorial State Park. Turn left, drive 4 miles and stop at the entrance to pay a small fee. Continue on the main road and park at the Visitor Center.

The trailhead is located behind the Visitor Center. The trail immediately begins climbing through desert vegetation including yucca, agave, ocotillo, sotol, and mesquite. The first section of trail climbs away from Dog Canyon on a steep, rocky trail. The views open along the way to include the white sand dunes on the floor of the Tularosa Valley, and in the morning, striking colors on the Organ and San Andres mountains on the other side of the basin. After a jog to the south, at mile 0.6 the trail finishes the intense climb on a broad bench that offers a bit of level walking.

The trail again approaches Dog Canyon. At mile 1.5, a side trail to Fairchild Spring angles off to the left. The climb intensifies, rising 400 feet over the next 0.5 mile to reach a lovely grassy flat. This flat has oaks, alligator junipers, cholla cacti, the unusual fragrant ash tree, and huge boulders tumbled from the cliffs that soar above. Ideal campsites can be found near the larger trees.

From the flat, descend into Dog Canyon to reach the stream for the first time. Water is available here, dropping from the mesas above through a series of waterfalls. Shady cottonwoods offer relief from the sun, and the ruins of a line cabin are found at streamside. To prevent further damage to this sensitive area, camping is not permitted along the stream.

Steep limestone walls of Dog Canyon

The trail continues from behind the line camp to ascend the steepest section of the canyon, the "eyebrow." After a switchback to the left, the trail crosses a narrow ledge high above the canyon floor. Great views down canyon open up, but hikers should keep their eyes on the trail. Climbing continually, the trail skirts around to a gap in the cliffs. Now paralleling a drainage to the left, the trail continues its steep climb to the flanks of Joplin Ridge about 4 miles from the start. Now a more moderate ascent, the trail swings east to meet the rough FR 90B descending from West Side Road. Return to the trailhead by the same route.

57 WILLIE WHITE CANYON

Managed by: Lincoln National Forest, Cloudcroft Ranger District
Distance: 8 miles, day hike
Elevation range: 8,200 to 9,300 feet
Elevation gain: 1,200 feet
Difficulty: moderate
Seasons: May to late October
Water: Bluff Springs
Map: USGS Bluff Springs 7.5' quadrangle
Interesting features: old railroad grades, Bluff Springs

A small logging line, the Alamogordo and Sacramento Mountain Railway began in Alamogordo and climbed 5,000 feet in 26 miles to reach Cloudcroft at the edge of the timber. The terrain required engineers to design massive trestles, such as the one still standing at Mexican Canyon along US 82 just outside Cloudcroft. In the woods, canyon

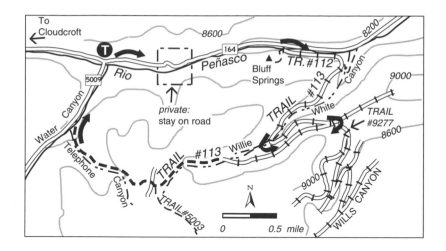

walls were crossed with ingenious switchbacking track that carried short logging trains over ridges and into uncut valleys. In 1924, rather than lay 20 miles of track in canyon bottoms, the railroad pushed tracks from the Rio Peñasco over a ridge to reach Willie White Canyon. Later, the company dropped rails into Wills Canyon, the next canyon south, on a series of precarious switchbacks. Slow-moving trains eased down a leg of track onto a short siding, then crawled backwards down the next switchback and siding, then moved forward down the next, and so on to the bottom.

Many of the graded railbeds have been converted into hiking trails. Except for the crossing of the saddle between Willie White and Telephone canyons, this hike is entirely on old railroad grades.

To reach the trailhead from Cloudcroft, take NM 130 south from the west end of town. In 2 miles, turn right onto NM 6563, which is signed for Sunspot. In about 8.5 miles, turn left onto FR 164, which is signed for Bluff Springs. Continue 2 miles to the intersection with FR 5009 to the right and park.

From the intersection, continue walking down FR 164 as the road follows an old railroad grade in a wide meadow bordering the headwaters of the Rio Peñasco. In 0.5 mile, stay on the road through a parcel of private land. At mile 1.5, come to the parking area for Bluff Springs. Turn right and explore this unusual area, climbing to the top of the bluff and perhaps to the spring 0.25 mile beyond. Return to the base of the bluff and find Trail No. 112 angling off to the southeast. This trail follows the old railroad grade heading into Willie White Canyon. Intersect Trail No. 113 in 0.5 mile from Bluff Springs and turn right. This trail continues on the railroad grade.

The trail soon swings southwest and heads up Willie White Canyon, passing through deep conifer forest. At mile 3.5, the trail crosses the bottom of Willie White Canyon. Here an old route continues up the canyon floor; the recently rerouted trail follows the railroad grade, angling to the left and climbing gradually on the canyon wall. After heading down canyon for 0.5 mile, Trail No. 113 intersects Trail No. 9277, remnants of another railroad grade that leads to switchbacks descending into Wills Canyon. Turn back sharply to the right to stay on Trail No. 113, which continues to follow a railroad grade, again heading up Willie White Canyon.

The wide trail climbs parallel to the canyon bottom, leaving the railroad grade and crossing the bottom about 5 miles from the start. Ignore the old trail along the canyon bottom and follow the new one as it climbs to the north canyon wall. At mile 5.8, reach the divide between Willie White Canyon and Telephone Canyon to the west. Here Trail No. 5003 goes left into Wills Canyon and a logging road follows along the crest. Continue straight and downhill on Trail No. 113. The trail quickly loses 700 feet over the next mile as it descends into Telephone Canyon, again in lush forest. At the junction with Water Canyon, Trail No. 113 ends at FR 5009. Turn right onto the road and walk 0.75 mile back to the trailhead.

Mexican Trestle is the most dramatic remnant of the logging railroads in the Sacramento Mountains.

58 THREE RIVERS PETROGLYPH SITE

Managed by: Bureau of Land Management, Las Cruces District
Distance: 3 miles, day hike
Elevation range: 5,000 to 5,200 feet
Elevation gain: 200 feet
Difficulty: easy
Seasons: all-year
Water: at the campground
Map: USGS Golindrina Draw 7.5' quadrangle
Interesting features: outstanding petroglyphs

Jornada-style petroglyphs are located at hundreds of sites across the desert regions of southern New Mexico. Related to the famous black-and-white Mimbres pottery style, these drawings are characterized by animal motifs, flat-headed human or god-like portraits, and complex geometric designs. A short hike along a lava cliff at the Three Rivers Petroglyph Site leads past an astounding array of hundreds of examples of this rock art. Bighorn sheep, horned lizards, fish, birds, spirals, and intertwining lines are pecked into the basalt. In a state where ancient rock art is a common feature, this is by far one of the most spectacular collections. The site and a campground are carefully managed by the Bureau of Land Management, and a small fee is collected for visiting the area.

To reach the trailhead, take FR 579, which is located off US 54 30 miles north of Alamogordo and 28 miles south of Carrizozo. Head east, following the signs for the Three Rivers Petroglyph Site and Three Rivers Campground. In 4.5 miles, turn left at the entrance to the petroglyph site.

From the trailhead, follow the path up to a low ridge, staying on the well-worn path as it climbs the basalt. At the black rocks, watch for the plentiful petroglyphs on just about any flat surface. Each branch of

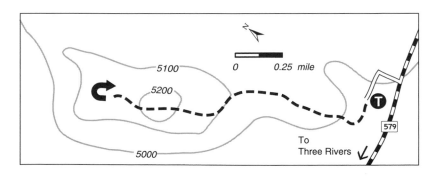

Geometric patterns are a common theme of the rock art at Three Rivers Petroglyph Site.

the trail leads to more pecked artwork, so plan on taking as many side trails as possible. The trail continues past the main group of rock art to a round knoll to the north and offers dramatic views of the Sierra Blanca to the east. On the return, hikers are certain to discover pictures they missed on the way up.

 # THREE RIVERS TRAIL

Managed by: Lincoln National Forest, White Mountain Wilderness, Smokey Bear Ranger District
Distance: 7 miles, day hike
Elevation range: 6,800 to 8,400 feet
Elevation gain: 1,600 feet
Difficulty: moderate
Seasons: April to November
Water: Three Rivers
Maps: USGS Godrey Peak and Nogal Peak 7.5' quadrangles, USFS White Mountain Wilderness
Interesting features: deep, quiet canyon; running water

In contrast with the sloping east side of the range, the rugged west face of the Sierra Blanca is a formidable barrier where the mountain front jumps 4,000 feet from base to crest. Three Rivers Canyon provides a route into the range from the west, an arduous trip by any

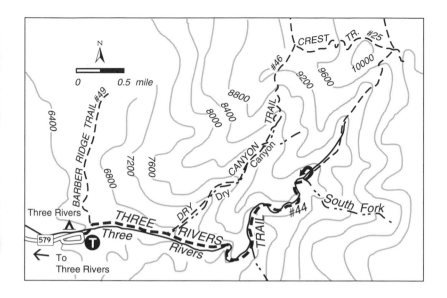

means. A day hike into the canyon is a delightfully wild experience that few take. The craggy canyon holds flowing water throughout, and hikers quickly leave behind the desert scrub of the foothills and enter shady conifer forest. Up to the junction with South Fork about 4 miles from the trailhead, pleasant campsites are plentiful, but hikers must resist the temptation to camp within 0.5 mile of the campground.

Those seeking a challenge can continue past the end of the described route and follow the Three Rivers Trail to the crest—ascending 4,000 feet—and return via the difficult Dry Canyon Trail No. 46. Check with the Smokey Bear District Ranger Station concerning trail conditions before attempting this difficult 12-mile loop.

To reach the trailhead, take FR 579 from Three Rivers, which is located off US 54 30 miles north of Alamogordo and 28 miles south of Carrizozo. Head east toward the Three Rivers Petroglyph Site and Three Rivers Campground. In 4.5 miles, pass the entrance to the petroglyph site, and in another mile, reach the end of the pavement. Stay on FR 579 by bearing right at mile 7.5 and left at mile 8.5, passing through private land. Continue to the campground, which is about 14 miles from US 54.

Begin hiking up canyon on Three Rivers Trail No. 44, which is located at the east end of the campground. Cross the stream on the main trail, avoiding the many side trails in the canyon bottom. The trail leads away from the shady trees onto the dry slopes, passing the Barber Ridge Trail No. 49. After passing through open stands of pine and Gambel's oak, the trail swings back near the stream and enters a shady pine and alligator juniper forest. Climb continuously along the stream, passing the Dry Canyon Trail No. 46 at mile 0.9. Along this stretch, the stream often disappears in the rocks. It is an unusual forest, with sparse understory and few wildflowers, but abundant campsites are available under the tall trees.

Reach a rocky stretch of trail with tall cliffs on either side of the canyon at mile 1.9. Bigtooth maple and little walnut (nogal) shade the stream here. After a series of bends, cross a dry side canyon and take a couple of short switchbacks to the base of a granite cliff. Beyond, the trail enters an open area that offers views of the main range. Continue another 0.5 mile to where the South Fork enters the main canyon, a convenient turnaround point.

60 BIG BONITO LOOP

Managed by: Lincoln National Forest, White Mountain Wilderness, Smokey Bear Ranger District
Distance: 9 miles, day hike or backpack
Elevation range: 7,800 to 10,000 feet
Elevation gain: 2,300 feet
Difficulty: moderate
Seasons: late April to November
Water: Bonito Creek, Bonito Seep
Maps: USGS Nogal Peak 7.5' quadrangle, USFS White Mountain Wilderness
Interesting features: quiet canyons, open grassland peaks, scenic views

The White Mountain Wilderness is one of the most attractive backcountry areas in New Mexico. The mountains are the highest range in southern New Mexico, with rounded, gentle hills along the crest that give the range its characteristic beauty. Montane grasslands, an unusual vegetation type found in only a few areas of the state, cover much of the crest, providing the chance to walk an open ridgeline with extensive views of the range itself and of the valley and

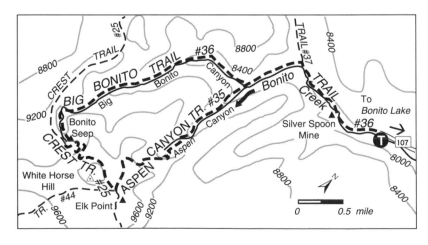

The headframe of the Silver Spoon Mine along the Big Bonito Trail

canyons below. The geology also creates a well-watered range with many springs found just below the crest. Campsites are plentiful in the grasslands.

To reach the trailhead, go 12 miles north of Ruidoso on NM 48 and turn left onto NM 37. After 1.3 miles, turn left onto FR 107, which is signed for Bonito Lake. Continue on this narrow, paved road past the lake and past South Fork Campground, where the pavement ends. Seven-and-a-half miles from NM 37, continue slowly through Bonito Riding Stables and reach the trailhead in another mile.

Trail No. 36, the Big Bonito Trail, immediately enters the wilderness as it crosses Argentina Canyon and begins to parallel Bonito Creek, heading upstream. Bee-balm, yarrow, mountain parsley, and Richardson geranium bloom here throughout the summer. The trail crosses the stream many times as it climbs steadily up the canyon floor. Pass the shaft and headframe of the Silver Spoon Mine at mile 0.7.

At mile 1, intersect the Little Bonito Trail No. 37. Bear left to stay on the Big Bonito Trail as the canyon turns abruptly south, offering a view of the not-too-distant crest. At mile 1.7, reach the junction with the Aspen Canyon Trail No. 35. The route returns to this junction later in the hike. Bear left onto the Aspen Canyon Trail and begin climbing in earnest. Beware of abundant stinging nettle close to the trail. Soon leave the forest behind and enter the grasslands, climbing several switchbacks. On the ascent, the views open to include Nogal Peak to the north and the Capitan Range to the east.

At a minor saddle near mile 3, turn right and continue climbing through a grassy bowl, gaining 500 feet to the next ridge. During the rainy season, the tread may disappear beneath a luxurious growth of alpine grass. Here the climb moderates, ascending the ridge to meet the Crest Trail No. 25 at mile 3.7 on a saddle between Elk Point to the east and White Horse Hill to the west.

From this high saddle, turn right onto the Crest Trail, skirting around the northern base of White Horse Hill. Drop quickly through several long switchbacks to Bonito Seep at mile 4.8. At the seep, pick up the south end of the Big Bonito Trail and drop into a grassy canyon that parallels the flow of water coming from Bonito Seep.

Beyond the grassy bowl near the crest, the trail loses altitude. Bonito Canyon is shady and cool much of the way, often thick with Gambel's oaks. The trail continues north for 1.5 miles before swinging to the east to meet the Aspen Canyon Trail at mile 7. At the junction, bear left and backtrack to the trailhead via the Big Bonito Trail, passing the Little Bonito Trail along the way.

61   ARGENTINA PEAK

Managed by: Lincoln National Forest, White Mountain Wilderness, Smokey Bear Ranger District
Distance: 6 miles, day hike or backpack
Elevation range: 7,800 to 9,100 feet
Elevation gain: 1,600 feet
Difficulty: moderate
Seasons: late April to November
Water: Spring Cabin Spring, Argentina Spring
Maps: USGS Nogal Peak 7.5' quadrangle, USFS White Mountain Wilderness
Interesting features: running water, old mines, extensive views

Argentina Peak is one of the easiest destinations along the crest of the White Mountains, and the views from the trail are no less

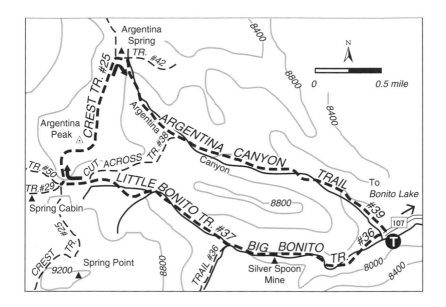

spectacular than those from other, higher locations. Cool and shady canyons lead up to and down from the grasslands along the crest, and water is available at several springs along the way. Campsites are limited along this route, but a few scenic spots are located along the crest and at Spring Cabin.

The trailhead for this hike is the same as for the Big Bonito Loop, hike No. 60. Begin hiking on the Big Bonito Trail No. 36, immediately crossing the wilderness boundary. About 0.75 mile from the start, pass the impressive remains of the headframe of the Silver Spoon Mine. At mile 1, come to the junction with the Little Bonito Trail No. 37. Bear right and continue climbing on Trail No. 37 above the stream. Pass several small clearings suitable for camping along the way.

After passing a faint trail leading to Little Bonito Spring, come to the intersection with the Cut Across Trail No. 38, a shortcut to Argentina Canyon that bypasses the wonderful views from the crest. Continue straight, soon entering a grassy meadow with views of flat-topped Spring Point to the left. At mile 2.3, arrive at a five-way intersection. Trail No. 29 leads west to Spring Cabin and its spring for those who need water or a quiet campsite. Turn right onto the Crest Trail No. 25, climbing steeply out of the saddle. Cross a small meadow that offers nice views to the south and west. The trail skirts the eastern base of Argentina Peak, with excellent views of the ridges of the northern Sierra Blanca. The views are increasingly grand as the trail drops from the north side of Argentina Peak and returns to the crest.

Intersect the Argentina Canyon Trail No. 39 at Argentina Spring at mile 3.4. Turn right onto Trail No. 39, bearing right again in 0.2 mile at the intersection with the Clear Water Trail No. 42. Parallel a small stream, now heading downhill, crossing the bottom of the

The grassy crest of Sierra Blanca

drainage several times. Again intersect the Cut Across Trail at mile 4.1 and continue downhill. About 2 miles from the crest, cross the wilderness boundary and reach the trailhead.

62 SOUTH FORK OF THE RIO BONITO

Managed by: Lincoln National Forest, White Mountain Wilderness, Smokey Bear Ranger District
Distance: 6 miles, day hike
Elevation range: 7,500 to 8,400 feet
Elevation gain: 1,000 feet
Difficulty: easy
Seasons: late April to November
Water: at the campground and along South Fork
Maps: USGS Nogal Peak 7.5' quadrangle, USFS White Mountain Wilderness
Interesting features: lush canyon, wild brook trout, running water

Hikers looking for something less taxing than a steep climb to the crest of the Sierra Blanca should try the South Fork of the Rio Bonito. The lower mile of this hike often receives heavy use on summer weekends but, above the wilderness boundary, hikers are likely to share the

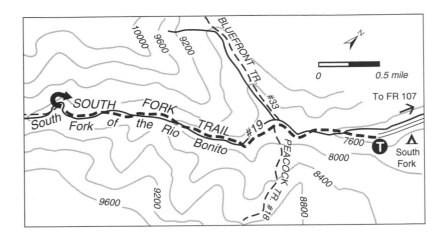

canyon only with elk, bear, and wild brook trout. Scenic campsites are located throughout the canyon bottom. The brook trout in the stream are voracious feeders although easily spooked in the clear water. For those out for more than a casual stroll, the South Fork Trail extends up to the crest where it joins the Bluefront Trail, creating a 12-mile, strenuous circuit with a 3,000-foot elevation gain, most of which comes in a 2-mile stretch.

To reach the trailhead, go 12 miles north of Ruidoso on NM 48 and turn left onto NM 37. After 1.3 miles, turn left onto FR 107, which is signed for Bonito Lake. Continue on this narrow, paved road past the lake 5 miles to the turnoff for South Fork Campground. Turn left and continue 0.75 mile to the trailhead at the campground.

Begin hiking at the end of the road at the South Fork Trail No. 19 sign. Immediately enter the deep, shady conifer forest where multiple routes lead up canyon. As the trail climbs away from the canyon bottom, look for sections of an old wooden pipe surrounded by banded metal that was part of a water system designed to deliver water to the railroad at Carrizozo, 30 miles away. After crossing to the south bank of the stream at the base of a tall granite cliff, pass the remains of the dam that supplied water to the pipe. Cross into the White Mountain Wilderness, where the trail narrows and sees fewer users. Intersect the Bluefront Trail No. 33 at mile 0.8 and bear left, climbing above the stream. After passing the Peacock Trail No. 18, drop back down to stream level and cross the stream where yellow thistles bloom in midsummer.

Continue up the narrowing canyon, always within earshot of the running water. The trail passes through small meadows, each offering quiet campsites. About 3 miles from the start, after crossing the stream several times, the trail rounds a broad bend in the stream at the base of a granite ridge, a good turnaround spot. Return to the trailhead by the same route.

Wild brook trout invite a bit of angling on the South Fork of the Rio Bonito. (Kevin Fabryka photo)

63   CAPITAN PEAK

Managed by: Lincoln National Forest, Capitan Wilderness, Smokey Bear
    Ranger District
Distance: 14 miles, day hike or backpack
Elevation range: 5,300 to 10,083 feet
Elevation gain: 4,700 feet
Difficulty: strenuous
Seasons: late April to October
Water: carry water
Map: USGS Arabela and Capitan Peak 7.5' quadrangles
Interesting features: unmatched views, challenging hike

    Rising 5,000 feet above the surrounding plains, the Capitan Mountains serve as a prominent landmark for travelers entering south-central New Mexico from the east or north. From the summit of the range on Capitan Peak, the expansive view takes in almost all of southeastern

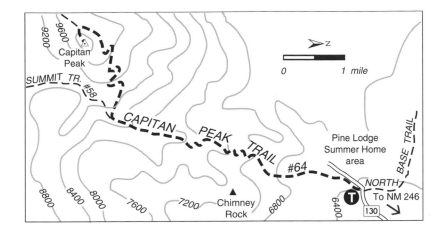

New Mexico from Texas to the southern Rockies. The rugged east side of the range is a little-visited wilderness area and, with the exception of the fall hunting season, hikers should enjoy a day of solitude on the way to the peak.

Be prepared for a long, arduous hike. Allow 7 to 12 hours to make the 14-mile round trip to the summit and back. No water is found along the route and, on a hot summer day, plan on carrying and drinking at least a gallon of fluid. Those seeking a less challenging trip can make the 4-mile round trip to Chimney Rock.

To reach the trailhead at the Pine Lodge Summer Home area, take NM 246 about 33 miles north and east of Capitan or about 50 miles west of Roswell. Turn south onto FR 130, a rough dirt road that often requires a high-clearance vehicle. Continue 4 miles, passing the North Base Trailhead on the right immediately before reaching the Capitan Peak Trailhead.

Begin hiking on the Capitan Peak Trail No. 64. The early part of the trail parallels FR 130, passing on the edge of the summer home area. In 0.25 mile, intersect a trail from the cabins coming in from the end of the road on the right. Stay on the main trail at a small drainage and, after crossing the Capitan Wilderness boundary, begin the long, steep climb. The trail follows a ridge through a low-growing juniper forest for the next 0.25 mile before making a short, steep climb at mile 1.

At the base of the first series of switchbacks at mile 1.5, the trail turns sharply to the right. Climb a long series of switchbacks ascending a narrow ridge, with glimpses of Chimney Rock through the trees to the left. At the top of the wiggles at mile 2, the trail offers fine views of Chimney Rock. This is a good turnaround point for those seeking an easy day hike.

The trail continues to follow a narrow ridge, with another set of intense switchbacks beginning at mile 3.1. In another 0.5 mile, the trail levels a bit, now traversing Douglas-fir forest. Pass a viewpoint of Sunset Peak to the east at mile 4.2.

171

Sunlight on grass

Just past mile 5, reach a T intersection with the Summit Trail No. 58. Bear right onto the Summit Trail, following the signs for Capitan Peak, which is 1.5 miles west. After a 0.5-mile traverse, the trail begins a series of broad switchbacks that lead to the summit ridge, where frequent openings in the trees offer views to the north. At mile 6.2, the trail swings below Capitan Peak. Continue climbing to a sloping meadow at mile 7 where a sign points the way to the summit. Turn left and cross the meadow, where a riot of wildflowers blooms all summer long. A few hundred yards lead to the peak and a glorious 360-degree view.

Campsites are scattered along the edge of the meadow below the summit. Return to the trailhead by the same route.

64   LAST CHANCE CANYON

Managed by: Lincoln National Forest, Guadalupe Ranger District
Distance: 10 miles, day hike or backpack
Elevation range: 4,500 to 5,200 feet
Elevation gain: 800 feet
Difficulty: moderate
Seasons: fall through late spring
Water: White Oak Spring, along Last Chance Canyon
Maps: USGS Red Bluff Draw and Queen 7.5' quadrangles
Interesting features: large springs, high canyon walls, solitude

The story of how this canyon got its name is told so often that it just might contain a kernel of truth. Around 1881, a group of ranchers pursued Apache raiders into the Guadalupe Mountains and soon became lost amid the twisted canyons draining the southeast flank of the range. After their canteens were empty, they rode from rim to rim,

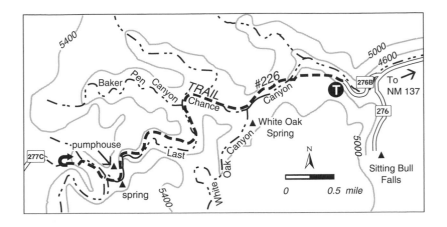

searching for water, without finding a spring. With their horses almost spent, they spotted the limestone walls of yet another canyon—it was their last chance. According to the legend, the abundant springs they found there saved their lives, and they named the spot Last Chance Canyon.

Just down the road from popular Sitting Bull Falls, Last Chance Canyon offers the last chance to escape the crowds at the falls and enter a lonesome, limestone wilderness, one of my favorite spots in all of New Mexico. A couple of miles up the canyon is a spring and travertine wall similar to the ones in Sitting Bull Canyon, but rarely visited. With abundant water and myriad side canyons to explore, Last Chance is an excellent place for an overnight stay.

The mouth of Last Chance Canyon is located near the Sitting Bull Falls Recreation Area off of NM 137. Twelve miles north of Carlsbad, turn west onto NM 137 and continue on this paved road about 24 miles to FR 276, the road to Sitting Bull Falls. Turn right and drive about 6.5 miles to FR 276B on the right. Turn and continue about 0.25 mile to the end of this rough road.

From the trailhead, walk up canyon on Trail No. 226, located on the south side of the canyon bottom. The towering limestone walls of the canyon are clothed in Torrey yuccas, sotol, bear grass, and prickly pear cactus, and the canyon is very wide in its lower reaches. At mile 1, drop into the canyon bottom shaded by some large hackberry trees, cross the stream, and pass through a gate.

As the canyon walls squeeze in against the canyon bottom, the trail crosses limestone ledges. Small ponds of clear water stand in the canyon bottom, flowing from White Oak Spring in the side canyon entering from the south. Listen for the incongruous trill of a belted kingfisher searching for minnows in a desert canyon. Soon pass a massive gray and orange wall of travertine deposited at the mouth of White Oak Canyon. The travertine cliff has many intricate faces and includes an unusual natural bridge on its western end.

Beyond White Oak Spring, Last Chance Canyon widens. Cross to the south side of the canyon bottom before the trail swings south along a bend in the canyon. At the mouth of Baker Pen Canyon entering from the right are several shady campsites. Near gray stair-step limestone ledges, the trail follows the rocky canyon bottom for a few yards before climbing to a bench above. Climb steeply through several switchbacks to cross a spur ridge. The trail is scratched into the slopes above the canyon floor.

The trail becomes difficult to follow as it turns south and begins to drop to some spring-fed ponds. When a route to the canyon bottom is clearly visible, drop down to the stream and walk up the rock ledges near the pools of clear water. Most of the pools are only a few inches deep, but one is a wonderful swimming hole over 6 feet deep. Flat benches along the stream offer idyllic camping spots.

Although the trail follows the north bank of the stream, it is easier and more interesting to follow the canyon bottom upstream. Continue in the stream bed around a couple of bends until reaching a deep pool

Flowing water supports lush vegetation in Last Chance Canyon, a striking contrast to the dry desert slopes. (United States Forest Service photo)

with intake water pipes leading to a small shed. Follow the pipe to pick up the trail again, passing the ruins of a tin pumphouse with rusting machinery inside. The trail passes a large spring, then crosses the stream bottom. In a minute, reach the junction of Last Chance with a side canyon entering from the right. Cross Last Chance and follow a trail heading up the small side canyon. At a minor junction, take the fork to the right. Climb the switchbacks leading up the south wall of the canyon until reaching the top of a knife-edge ridge. Peek over the edge to the left for another view of Last Chance Canyon. Return to the trailhead by the same route.

65 SITTING BULL FALLS

Managed by: Lincoln National Forest, Guadalupe Ranger District
Distance: 7 miles, day hike
Elevation range: 4,660 to 5,725 feet
Elevation gain: 1,100 feet
Difficulty: moderate
Seasons: all year
Water: Sitting Bull Falls, Sitting Bull Spring
Map: USGS Queen 7.5' quadrangle
Interesting features: running water, unusual waterfall

Sitting Bull, a Dakota Sioux from the northern Great Plains, probably never set foot in New Mexico. But a much-repeated legend claims that cowboys chased a group of Indians that included the old chief into Sitting Bull Canyon and thereby discovered the falls. Unfortunately for the story, Sitting Bull was in Canada in 1881, the year of the reputed discovery.

An equally improbable explanation tells of early Eddy County resident Bill Jones spinning tales of the old days in the Guadalupes. His description of the falls was met with derisive comments from his brothers, who

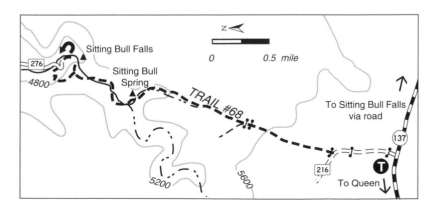

Sitting Bull Falls

called it "pure bull." "Well, Sitting Bull," suggested one brother, "if those falls are really there, we'll name them after you!"

One can drive to the base of Sitting Bull Falls, but dropping in from the mesa above makes the trip a memorable one. This longer hike begins on NM 137 and drops into Sitting Bull Canyon, passing along the way the spring that is the source of the water that trickles through matted green and red plants to create this unusual waterfall.

To reach the trailhead, take NM 137 from US 285 north of Carlsbad. In about 24 miles, continue straight when the road to Sitting Bull Falls goes right. Climb the escarpment and enter the Lincoln National Forest, passing the U.S. Forest Service's Guadalupe Work Center about 11 miles from the falls intersection. Continue about 1 mile to a sign for Trail No. 68 on the right side of the road.

Begin Trail No. 68 by walking through a gate on a primitive road. After 0.4 mile, pass through another gate. In a few hundred yards, the road, here marked FR 216, bears left. Bear right through a gate on what is now identified as Trail No. 68. At mile 1.5, the trail reaches two gates within 50 feet of each other. At an intersection 50 feet beyond the second gate, take the right fork. Soon the trail parallels a deep draw on the left. A low rock wall marks where the trail turns left to enter the draw, which soon deepens into a full-fledged canyon. Enjoy the views down canyon and of the plains in the distance as you descend, but watch out for loose rocks.

About 2 miles from the start, reach the bottom of the canyon and cross to the west side. The trail now meanders across the canyon bottom. As the trail swings west, pass Sitting Bull Spring on the right. From here down, clear, running water is found in the stream bottom. Descend a bit more into the bottom of a large canyon, bear right and pass through a hiker gate. Continue downstream, arriving at a trail junction 3 miles from the start. First, bear right and take the short spur trail to see the top of the falls, then return to the junction and continue down the cliff on the trail marked for FR 276. At the bottom of the hill, reach a parking lot, cross to the east side, and pick up the trail leading to the bottom of the falls. Enjoy the falls from below, then return to the trailhead by the same route.

66   LONESOME RIDGE

Managed by: Lincoln National Forest, Guadalupe Ranger District
Distance: 12 miles, day hike or backpack
Elevation range: 6,600 to 7,200 feet
Elevation gain: 1,400 feet
Difficulty: strenuous
Seasons: March to May, September to December
Water: carry water
Maps: USGS El Paso Gap and Gunsight Canyon 7.5' quadrangles
Interesting features: lonesome feeling, rugged canyon country, wildlife viewing

The smooth face of the west edge of the Guadalupe Mountains is most dramatically contrasted by the eastern rim, which is made of a series of ridges jutting like fingers from the hand of Guadalupe Ridge. Walking any of the narrow ridges presents grand views into the deeply incised canyons of the rim, a thousand-foot section of limestone piled

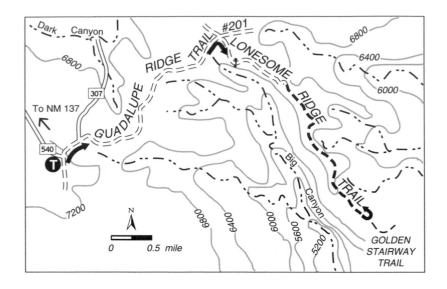

on top of more limestone. The Lonesome Ridge Trail leaves Guadalupe Ridge and crosses narrow saddles and ridges before ending at the head of the Golden Stairway, a steep trail that drops from the rim to private land below.

The trailhead is a long way from the nearest town, but water and supplies are available along NM 137. Guadalupe National Forest has a water tap for campers and hikers at its Guadalupe Work Station located about 35 miles from US 285 on NM 137. Basic supplies and gas are available at Queen, just beyond the work center. Primitive camping is permitted along NM 137 and FR 540, including a large, wooded area suitable for group camping at the trailhead.

To get to the trailhead, take NM 137 west from US 285 about 12 miles north of Carlsbad. In 24 miles, pass the road to Sitting Bull Falls. Thirty-eight miles from the highway, pass the Queen store on the right. Three-and-a-half miles past the store, turn left onto the gravel FR 540. This is an excellent all-weather gravel road. In 0.5 mile, bear right, and continue about 12 miles to the end of the gravel road.

Begin hiking north (left) on Trail No. 201, the Guadalupe Ridge Trail, which is actually a jeep road. In 0.25 mile, pass FR 307 on the left. Continue on the narrow ridge, making repeated climbs and descents, with glimpses of Big Canyon to the right and upper Dark Canyon on the left. The road surface is rocky, with sharp limestone underfoot. The pine and juniper forest is occasionally broken by areas of recent fire, a common feature in the hot, dry Guadalupes. At mile 1.8, Lonesome Ridge comes into view on the right.

Three miles from the start, arrive at a four-way intersection. Take the rightmost fork onto Lonesome Ridge. At mile 3.4, views open up to the Big Canyon system. At a gate, bear left and pass through it. After the road crosses a saddle, there are excellent views in all directions. Continue on the road to just beyond mile 4.1 where the road suddenly narrows into a trail. Skirt the edge of a broad bowl of limestone, peeking over the edge for more views of Big Canyon. Cairns mark the trail as it circles the top of the ridge, then drops into a drainage heading toward the entrance to the Golden Stairway Trail. Continue about a mile farther along the very edge of Big Canyon, whose jagged cliffs offer a stunning backdrop to the trail.

Several rocky but flat areas are found on the extreme end of Lonesome Ridge, offering exposed campsites as a base for further exploration of the canyons, and from which to descend the Golden Stairway Trail. Turn around at the edge of Big Canyon or continue to the head of the Golden Stairway. The rocky descent into Big Canyon on this trail is for strong, experienced hikers only. Private land at the bottom forces those making the trip to retrace their steps along Lonesome Ridge.

The east face of the Guadalupe Escarpment from Lonesome Ridge

67 DEVILS DEN CANYON

Managed by: Lincoln National Forest, Guadalupe Ranger District
Distance: 6 miles, day hike
Elevation range: 6,400 to 7,200 feet
Elevation gain: 1,000 feet
Difficulty: moderate
Seasons: March to May, September to December
Water: Devils Den Spring
Map: USGS El Paso Gap 7.5' quadrangle
Interesting features: remote, spectacular canyon

In a dry land with only a thin veneer of unfriendly vegetation, the devil gets blamed for everything. The Southwest has more devil's canyons, stairways, thrones, peaks, and ridges than one can count. Devils Den Canyon is a rugged gorge slashed through the western rim of the Guadalupes, ending in a spectacular pour off along the mountain front. In the surrounding hills, a large herd of mule deer supports a small population of mountain lions. Watch for large cat prints in the soft sand.

The trailhead for the Devils Den Canyon Trail is the same as for the Lonesome Ridge Hike (No. 66). Note that a trailhead for a different Devils Den Trail is located on FR 540 about 2 miles north of the starting point for this hike. The second Devils Den Trail does not connect with the trail described here.

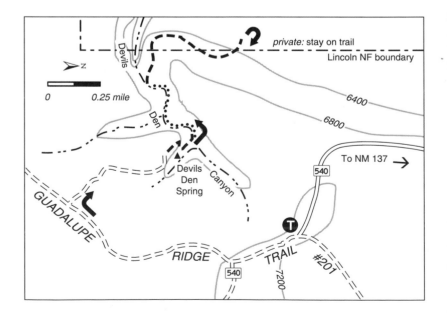

From the end of the gravel FR 540, continue south (right) on Trail No. 201, the Guadalupe Ridge Trail, which is actually a jeep road, but too rough for most vehicles beyond the first 0.25 mile. At an intersection at mile 0.3, bear right to stay on Trail No. 201. For the next 0.25 mile, pass through a maze of intertwined tracks heading up a rocky hill. Stay left, reaching a shallow stock tank at mile 0.6. Continue across a narrow ridge with the Big Canyon system on the left and the Devils Den Canyon on the right. At mile 1.2, in the middle of an easy climb, turn right onto an unmarked road to the right. This road is as wide as the Guadalupe Ridge Trail at this point but soon narrows. At another intersection in a few hundred feet, bear right, gradually dropping downhill on the rocky and rutted road surface, passing a large Texas madrone tree, recognized by its smooth red branches.

Fossils are common in the limestones of the Guadalupe Mountains.

At mile 1.7, the road ends at the ruins of a cabin above Devils Den Spring. Follow the trail past the cabin, reaching a fork. Take the right branch, which drops steeply on several switchbacks to the bottom of a side canyon just down from the spring. The trail continues to the mouth of the side canyon, then swings west into Devils Den Canyon. At first above the canyon floor, the trail soon drops to the rocky stream-bed. From here, walking in the canyon floor is much more interesting than taking the trail.

After passing a side canyon entering from the left, walk through a horseshoe bend. On the other side, flat ground and shady junipers invite camping for a day. At mile 2.4, a rock cairn (often made with three slabs of orange limestone) marks the trail's exit from the canyon. (A worthwhile side trip continues another 0.25 mile in the canyon bottom to a spectacular pour off about 200 feet high.) Turn right and climb out of the canyon bottom on the trail, entering private land.

Climb the north wall of the canyon to a saddle on a narrow spur ridge, making certain to stay on the trail in this area. At mile 2.6, the pour off in the canyon is visible to the left. After rounding a turn and heading north, the trail is perched on a ledge high above the floor of the canyon where views are outstanding. Follow the shelf trail until it fades away on a saddle at mile 3. Turn around and return by the same route.

68 LONGVIEW SPRING

Managed by: Carlsbad Caverns National Park
Distance: 6 miles, day hike or backpack
Elevation range: 4,550 to 6,000 feet
Elevation gain: 1,600 feet
Difficulty: moderate
Seasons: fall through late spring
Water: Longview Spring
Map: USGS Grapevine Draw 7.5' quadrangle
Interesting features: rugged canyon, long-range views, solitude

Although spectacular, Carlsbad Caverns can leave visitors eager for an escape from the crowds. One solution is to hike one of the park's backcountry trails, such as the Yucca Canyon Trail. Few make the trip to this distant corner park, and hikers will most likely have about 10 square miles of desert mountains to themselves. Permits are not required for day hiking in the backcountry, but hikers planning an overnight stay need to stop at the Carlsbad Caverns Visitor Center for a free permit.

The Guadalupe Mountains are one of the world's largest organically created structures. The entire range—and indeed a much more extensive, mostly buried, limestone structure over 300 miles long—is a fossil reef formed at the margin of a shallow arm of the sea during the Permian period, about 250 million years ago. The reef is made from the secretions of calcareous algae and the remains of sponges, bryozoans, brachiopods, and other shelled invertebrates. Over millions of years, these plants and animals grew on the remains of their ancestors, building a pile of lime almost 2,000-feet thick.

A walk up Yucca Canyon is also a climb through the reef. At first glance, the limestone layers appear to be homogenous. However, a close examination along the trail's transect of the canyon shows that each layer—ranging in thickness from a few inches to a couple

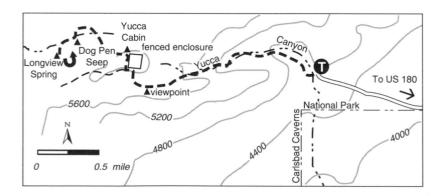

hundred feet—has its own characteristics. Specific fossils are common in one layer but not the next. The texture of the limestone also changes from massive to thinly laminated layers. Some layers are tinted red and include more sand than lime, an indication of a period when the reef was exposed above sea level.

To reach the trailhead, go south on US 62/180 from Whites City. In about 5 miles, turn right onto a paved county road which is signed for Slaughter Canyon Cave. Follow the signs for the cave about 10 miles to a fence at the National Park boundary. Turn left onto a rocky double track heading west parallel to the fence. This road is rough but is regularly driven by low-slung cars. Continue about 2 miles to the trailhead.

From the parking area, the trail immediately drops, crosses the stream bed, and turns up the canyon. The limestone of the Capitan reef is found in every direction, forming canyon walls over 1,500 feet high. The trail climbs steadily on the south wall of the canyon high above the bottom. At mile 0.7, again cross the canyon bottom. The trail frequently switches between the north and south walls, and the climb

A huge pile of limestone: the Guadalupe Mountains

is considerably steeper. The narrowing canyon supports alligator juniper and Texas madrone, which provide occasional shelter from the sun. A series of switchbacks leads high above the canyon floor, then the trail drops back to stream level. Atop the ridge at mile 1.5, the view to the south is never-ending and includes the southern portion of the Guadalupe Mountains in Texas and the rolling hills of the Pecos Valley.

Once on top of the ridge, the trail is more difficult to follow. Look for the faint tread heading north and for small cairns along the path. The trail leads to a large fenced enclosure among the piñon pine and juniper of the mesa top. Follow the south edge of the fence, then the west edge, to reach Yucca Cabin, ignoring a prominent trail angling from the southwest corner of the enclosure. From the cabin, cairns mark the trail west, first along the ridge top, then dropping into a small drainage. At the bottom, pass a rock corral and muddy spot called Dog Pen Seep. The trail continues down the drainage bottom, then up on the south side of the drainage wall. Soon the trail follows a ledge high above a larger canyon, swinging south. The Longview Spring is a few hundred feet farther on. By now it should be obvious how the spring got its name: the view into West Slaughter Canyon is spectacular. Return to the trailhead by the same route.

GILA RIVER REGION

The Catwalk is suspended from the rock walls of Whitewater Canyon.

69 FRISCO BOX

Managed by: Gila National Forest, Luna Ranger District
Distance: 6 miles, day hike or backpack
Elevation range: 6,400 to 6,600 feet
Elevation gain: 300 feet
Difficulty: easy
Seasons: late April to October
Water: San Francisco River
Map: USGS Dillon Mountain 7.5' quadrangle
Interesting features: hot springs, narrow box canyon

Box canyons—gorges so steep and rugged that they become impassable—offer first-class adventures for hikers. The San Francisco River is a major stream draining the northern portion of the Gila River region, and its box canyon is a classic example. Most of the river valley is filled with wide, grassy meadows but, at the Box, the river flows through a ridge of erosion-resistant granite. The water tumbles over the granite boulders, creating deep pools between sheer walls.

Hiking into the Box requires a good deal of wading and at times some swimming. High water in spring makes the river crossings difficult, and water temperatures can be surprisingly cold in October; it is best to hike in the Frisco Box in summer. Old running shoes are the ideal footwear for the hike. Backpackers should plan to camp in the meadows along the river before reaching the Box, and should always keep a watchful eye on the level of the river. Summer storms in far-off mountains can send a flash flood down the canyon. Before starting off on this hike, check with the District Ranger in Luna for road and stream conditions.

Getting to the trailhead is more arduous than the hike itself, and the trip requires a four-wheel drive vehicle. From Luna, take FR 19 north from town. Continue about 5 miles and turn right onto FR 210. This

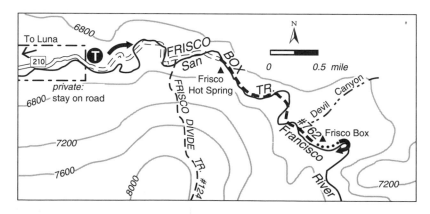

A stream in the dry Gila River Region (Bob Julyan photo)

rough road crosses many sandy stream beds that are difficult when dry and should not be attempted when water is running in them. Most of the road is on private land. Be sure to stay on the road and close all gates you open. Eight miles from FR 19, reenter public land and park.

From the parking area, begin walking on the road, which is also designated as the Frisco Box Trail No. 762, as it climbs steeply over a low saddle. The trail descends back to river level and continues along the grassy valley, heading downstream. The road makes four river crossings over the next mile. The slopes of the canyon are covered with conifers, and in summer, the valley floor is carpeted with wildflowers. After rounding a long horseshoe bend, intersect the Frisco Divide Trail No. 124 at mile 1.4. In another 0.5 mile, reach the end of the road at Frisco Hot Spring.

Hikers with cold feet can warm them in the pools at the spring. Continue along the river, now on a trail. At mile 2.6, the river turns sharply to the east before being joined by Devil Canyon. The dramatic entrance to the Box lies just beyond the next turn.

Hiking is more challenging beyond the entrance to the Box. Hikers will need to pick their route with care, boulder hopping much of the way. It is often difficult to wade through pools surrounded by large boulders; some deeper pools require swimming. About 0.5 mile into the Box, only skilled climbers can pass a large mid-stream boulder. Hikers should turn around at this point and return to the trailhead by the same route.

70   PUEBLO CREEK

Managed by: Gila National Forest, Luna Ranger District
Distance: 9 miles, day hike or backpack
Elevation range: 5,800 to 6,200 feet
Elevation gain: 500 feet
Difficulty: easy
Seasons: March to November
Water: carry water
Map: USGS Saliz Pass 7.5' quadrangle
Interesting features: minerals, isolated mountain scenery

The little-used Blue Range Wilderness abuts the Arizona-New Mexico border, part of the larger Blue Range Primitive Area. The area receives only a few hundred visitors each year, helping to make this hike lovely from spring to fall. The isolated canyon of Pueblo Creek cuts through the wilderness, and the WS Mountain Trail No. 43 follows the canyon about 9 miles to WS Lake. Additional trails met along

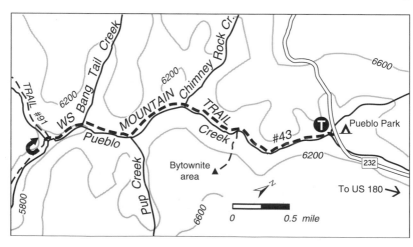

Red skimmer dragonfly

the way lead into Arizona. A rock outcrop on the east side of the canyon yields shiny bytownite crystals, a translucent mineral often cut into gems. The mineral is found scattered on the ground along a faint trail that leaves from the canyon bottom around mile 1.2 and lesser quantities are found along Pueblo Creek.

To reach the trailhead from Glenwood, take US 180 north about 27 miles to the junction with FR 232. Turn left and drive this good gravel road 5.6 miles to Pueblo Park Campground. The trailhead is just across the road.

Begin hiking south on the WS Mountain Trail No. 43. The rugged trail follows the canyon bottom and is sporadically marked with rock cairns. Watch carefully for markers as the trail swings from bank to bank, or simply follow the floor of the canyon and pick up the trail whenever it is found. The canyon narrows at mile 0.4 where walking is easier on the trail just above the canyon floor in the forest of ponderosa pine and alligator juniper. At mile 1.2, watch carefully for a faint trail heading to the bytownite crystal area or search for minerals along the main stream.

The canyon broadens near Chimney Rock Canyon, which enters at mile 2.2 from the west. Water usually flows in the creek bottom below this point. Continue down the benches under the canopy of broad-leaved trees. Mesas of juniper and piñon pine rise higher above the canyon floor as small side streams enter from east and west and water flows in the canyon bottom. Fine campsites are located near the confluences with Pup Creek at mile 3.1 and Bang Tail Creek at mile 4. At the junction with the Tige Canyon Trail No. 91 at mile 4.5, turn around to return by the same route or camp and further explore up Tige Canyon or along Bear Creek a mile below.

71 WHITEWATER BALDY

Managed by: Gila National Forest, Gila Wilderness, Glenwood Ranger District
Distance: 12 miles, day hike or backpack
Elevation range: 9,100 to 10,895 feet
Elevation gain: 1,900 feet
Difficulty: strenuous
Seasons: mid-May to November
Water: Bead Spring and Hummingbird Spring
Maps: USGS Grouse Mountain 7.5' quadrangle, USFS Gila Wilderness
Interesting features: fine views, deep forest

The Crest Trail No. 182 is well-used and easy to follow as it ascends a high ridge from the trailhead to Hummingbird Saddle and beyond to the summit of Mogollon Baldy, 12 miles away. A shorter trip leads to the summit of Whitewater Baldy; at 10,895 feet it is the highest point in the Mogollon Range. Because water and campsites are readily available at Hummingbird Saddle, this hike is popular. The route leads through a deep Douglas-fir forest and offers some wonderful views of the Gila Region. The trail is exposed all along the ridge, so hikers should be prepared for severe weather. Plan to be off the summit of Whitewater Baldy during storms, which are likely most summer afternoons. Note that some snow may linger on the higher sections of this trail until early June.

To reach the trailhead, drive about 4 miles north of Glenwood on US 180 and turn right onto NM 159. Take this winding road past the town of Mogollon, where it becomes FR 28, and continue about 18 miles from the highway to the Sandy Point Trailhead.

Begin hiking south on the Crest Trail No. 182 toward Hummingbird Saddle and Mogollon Baldy. The trail begins a moderate climb through Douglas-fir forest, a shady walk even in summer. Although moderate,

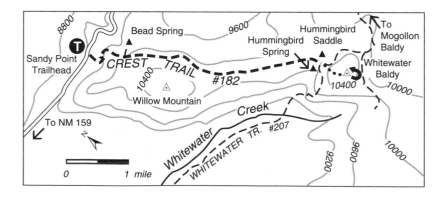

Ladybugs covering pine branches are a common sight on mountain summits.

the climb is constant for the first 1.5 miles. Watch for occasional views back toward Mineral Creek on the ascent. As the climb levels at mile 1.6, enter the Gila Wilderness. A short spur trail to the left leads to the lush Bead Spring. Resume the ascent as the trail swings to the east of Willow Mountain before gaining the ridge at a low saddle at mile 2.5. Continue along the rolling ridgeline, climbing to a knoll above Hummingbird Saddle at mile 4.2. From the knoll, the view west is down Whitewater Creek. Drop down to Hummingbird Saddle at mile 4.9, where water from the nearby spring and plenty of fine campsites are found.

A faint, unofficial trail leads south from the saddle to the summit of Whitewater Baldy straight ahead. Follow the trail along the shoulder of the crest, climbing steeply and slowly in the thin air. On the summit, head around to the south side where the view extends far south to the Gila River canyons. Return to the trailhead by the same route.

72 THE CATWALK AND BEYOND

Managed by: Gila National Forest, Glenwood Ranger District
Distance: 5 miles, day hike
Elevation range: 5,100 to 5,800
Elevation gain: 1,000 feet
Difficulty: easy
Seasons: mid-March through November
Water: Whitewater Creek
Maps: USGS Holt Mountain and Mogollon 7.5' quadrangles, USFS Gila Wilderness
Interesting features: deep, narrow canyon, historic pipeline, unique trail

The Catwalk National Recreation Trail is one of the most unusual hikes to be found anywhere in the Southwest. The route follows that of a pipeline constructed to supply water to a mining mill and town located at the mouth of Whitewater Canyon. The town of Graham was founded in 1893, just after the discovery of rich ore within the canyon. Although water always flowed within the canyon, Whitewater Creek was often dry at the townsite. The solution was to run a 4-mile pipe to carry water from within the canyon. As one might guess from its name, the canyon is a narrow gorge of tumbling water. The pipeline (and hence the trail) was often forced to cling to the rock walls. In the narrowest section, the pipe was suspended above the stream supported by spikes driven into the rocks. The precarious pipeline was difficult to maintain, and miners were often forced to walk the line to fix leaks. Their balancing act gave the pipeline the name "catwalk."

The gold and silver mines were worked for 20 years, closing down in 1913. In 1935, the route of the pipeline was converted into a walking

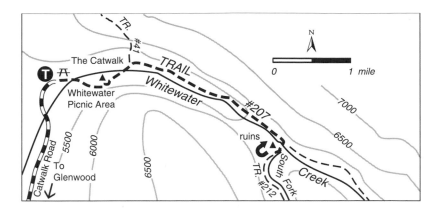

trail by the Civilian Conservation Corps. The trail maintains the unique design of the pipeline, frequently traveling above the raging water on steel grates and following the serpentine turns of the canyon, which in places is only 10 feet wide. Where the canyon widens, the route is scraped onto the cliffs high above the rapids.

From Silver City, take US 180 west for 62 miles to the town of Glenwood. Turn right at the signed intersection onto Catwalk Road and continue for 5 miles to the Whitewater Picnic Area. The road fords Whitewater Creek twice, the second time right at the picnic area. During spring runoff or after summer thunderstorms, these fords may be impassable. Call ahead to the Glenwood Ranger Station (505-539-2481) to check on road conditions.

The trail begins on the left (north) side of the creek at the Gila National Forest's Whitewater Picnic Area. The first mile of the trail cuts through the narrowest portion of the gorge on a series of stairs, bridges, narrow ledges, and metal grates. Because of narrow passages, hikers with backpacks will find this section of trail challenging. The roar of the water is constant. Sections of the 18-inch pipe are scattered about, and bolts and concrete piers that once supported the pipeline are visible in many places.

About 1 mile from the start, the Catwalk Trail crosses a suspension bridge and ends on a narrow ledge. Just before the bridge, turn left at the sign marking Trail No. 207. The trail climbs for a short distance to intersect Trail No. 41 at mile 1.2. After returning to stream level, watch for sections of the pipeline that once carried water down the canyon. At mile 1.4, the route climbs and descends several steep hills on the north bank of the stream. Fishing is excellent along this stretch, particularly in the fall. Groves of tall pines offer ideal lunch spots near the water.

At mile 2.4, come to the intersection with Trail No. 212 where the South Fork meets Whitewater Creek. Bear right onto Trail No. 212, cross the stream, and look for the remains of a power generating station at the confluence. Fine campsites are found under the large trees. Return to the trailhead by the same route.

73 WOOD HAUL ROAD NATIONAL RECREATION TRAIL

Managed by: Gila National Forest, Silver City Ranger District
Distance: 7 miles, day hike
Elevation range: 6,250 to 7,350 feet
Elevation gain: 1,200 feet
Difficulty: moderate
Seasons: all year
Water: carry water
Map: USGS Ft. Bayard 7.5' quadrangle
Interesting features: long-range views, historic road, wagon ruts

At the foot of the Pinos Altos Range, Fort Bayard was established as a frontier cavalry post in 1866. Because the post was located in open woodlands, large quantities of firewood had to be hauled down from the surrounding mountains. A steep road was built into the timber, and carefully driven wagons were used to haul the felled pines. Some sections of the road were so steep that wagon wheels had to be locked with ropes and the wagons dragged down the slope. Deeply etched wagon ruts are found along the trail today. The trail passes through a state-operated elk range, and hikers should watch for large herds in the woodlands.

From Central, which is located on US 180 8 miles east of Silver City, take the well-marked Fort Bayard Road north through the Fort Bayard Medical Center to FR 536. Continue north another 3.2 miles to a road marked for the Wood Haul Road Trailhead. Turn left and continue 0.2 mile to the trailhead parking area.

Begin hiking west on the trail as it passes through open juniper-piñon woodland. In 0.6 mile, the trail crosses Stephens Creek, then in a few

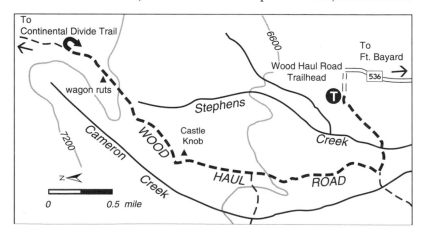

hundred yards it turns right onto the wagon road heading north. Climb gradually on the wide road. At mile 1.7, bear right at a trail junction or take a 1-mile side trip to Big Tree to the left.

The trail skirts the west flank of Castle Knob before entering a drainage. At mile 2.7, bear right and begin climbing a ridge at the foot of the Pinos Altos Range. As the trail cuts across the slope of the ridge, watch for the deep ruts worn into the rocks by wagons that were heavily loaded with ponderosa pines. After the trail levels a bit, reach a saddle at mile 3.5. The trail continues another 5 miles to the Continental Divide Trail, but this saddle makes a good turnaround point.

Circus beetle

74 MIDDLE FORK/ LITTLE BEAR LOOP

Managed by: Gila National Forest, Gila Wilderness, Wilderness Ranger District
Distance: 12 miles, backpack
Elevation range: 5,800 to 6,400 feet
Elevation gain: 600 feet
Difficulty: moderate
Seasons: April to October
Water: Middle Fork of the Gila River
Maps: USGS Woodland Park, Burnt Corral Canyon, and Little Turkey Park 7.5' quadrangles, USFS Gila Wilderness
Interesting features: wild canyon scenery, hot springs

Aldo Leopold roamed the Gila National Forest in the 1910s as a forest ranger, and the wild character of the landscape motivated him to develop the idea of preserving such areas as untouched by man. In 1924, 755,000 acres of the Gila was set aside as the world's first wilderness area. Although the area is not as pristine as Leopold may have wished, the Gila has much to offer. Wild mountain scenery and abundant wildlife attract many visitors, but many hikers find the canyons of the Gila its most appealing feature.

Of the three major headwaters of the Gila River, the Middle Fork has the best scenery and trout fishing. The Middle Fork Trail follows

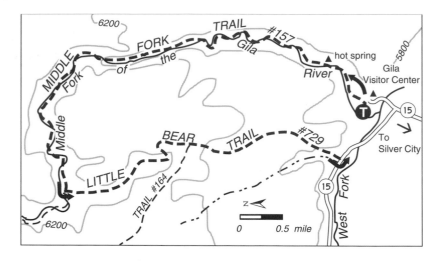

the river over 30 miles, offering the opportunity for a 6- or 7-day trip. High, rocky walls dominate a hike through the narrow canyon, and groves of lush riparian vegetation—sycamores, hackberries, and cottonwoods—provide relief from the open juniper woodlands that surround the gorge. Hot springs and good trout fishing in the spring and fall add to the appeal of the Middle Fork.

Hiking along the river is no easy feat. Frequent stream crossings, as many as six per mile, are tiring at low water but impossible during spring runoff and following heavy summer storms. The trail itself experiences frequent washouts and is often difficult to find. Sand and loose cobbles are apt to tire hikers faster than walking on a smooth trail. Plan on at least 10 hours of walking to complete this loop, and add more time to enjoy the many attractions of the canyon. Take advantage of numerous fine campsites found along the canyon floor. Before starting on a hike in the Middle Fork Canyon, contact the Wilderness Ranger District for current conditions. Hikers should carry a pair of running shoes to wear on the stream crossings.

From the intersection of NM 90 and US 180 in Silver City, go east on US 180 1 mile to the junction with Pinos Altos Road, NM 15. Turn left and travel the very winding and slow NM 15 through the Gila National Forest. In 22 miles, continue straight on NM 15 at the intersection with NM 35. Forty-three miles from Silver City, park in the backcountry area at the Gila Visitor Center.

Begin hiking up the canyon of the Middle Fork on the well-marked Middle Fork Trail No. 157. The wide canyon quickly narrows as the trail descends from a bench to meet the river. After the first of many stream crossings, the trail stays close to the river, passing through the grasses on the bank. At mile 1.1, beyond the second river crossing, look for a small hot spring located right on the riverbank. The canyon narrows as the walls grow steep, cutting off the rest of the world from view. Continue on the east side of the river, making another crossing

Rock spires tower above the Gila Forks. (Bob Julyan photo)

at mile 1.9. Here the river and trail are squeezed by the canyon walls, forcing the trail to cross the river frequently in the next mile.

As it passes through riparian areas in the next 2 miles, the trail is often difficult to follow. Hikers should find the easiest route upstream to mile 5.5 where the trail is more predominant. This is the wettest stretch of the route. As the trail swings west at mile 6, good campsites are found away from the river.

At mile 6.5, intersect the Little Bear Trail No. 729. Turn left onto the Little Bear Trail and begin climbing through a narrow canyon. Exit the canyon at mile 7.1 and continue an easy climb to a saddle above the canyon of the Middle Fork. Near the saddle at mile 8, pass the junction with the Woodland Park Trail No. 164. The trail descends across open juniper woodland to reach NM 15 and the trailhead for the Little Bear Trail at mile 10.2. To return to the Gila Visitor Center, turn left and walk along the road 1.2 miles.

75 BLACK RANGE CREST TRAIL

Managed by: Gila National Forest, Aldo Leopold Wilderness, Mimbres Ranger District
Distance: 10.5 miles one-way, day hike or backpack
Elevation range: 7,100 to 10,000 feet
Elevation gain: 2,100 feet
Difficulty: moderate
Seasons: April to October
Water: carry water
Maps: USGS Hillsboro Peak 7.5' quadrangle, USFS Aldo Leopold Wilderness
Interesting features: fine views

The huge Aldo Leopold Wilderness spans the crest of the Black Range from near Emory Pass to Diamond Peak 25 miles to the north. The wilderness boasts an extensive network of trails that sees few hikers. The trail to Hillsboro Peak follows the southern border of the wilderness and offers fine views into the wilder reaches of the Black Range. The views along the Crest Trail and from the peak itself make this hike a New Mexico classic.

The trailhead is at Emory Pass on NM 152. Reach the pass via NM 152 31 miles west of Interstate 25 and about 33 miles east of Central. Park at the Emory Pass Vista. Hikers wishing to do this hike as described should leave a second vehicle at the Gallinas Canyon Trailhead at Railroad Campground about 5 miles to the west on NM 152.

Begin hiking on a dirt road marked as the Crest Trail No. 79. Follow the road past a helispot and continue through a gate where the road becomes a trail. Begin a moderate climb that remains steady most of

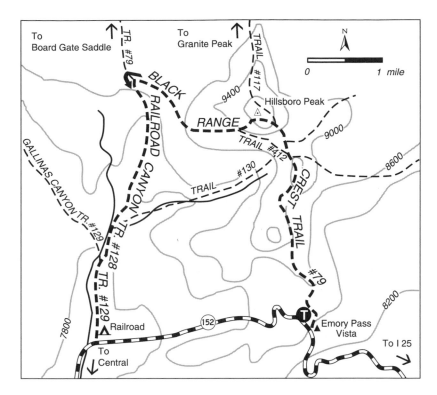

the way to the peak, passing through open conifer forest that offers frequent views to the north and east. At mile 1.9, enter the Aldo Leopold Wilderness and continue climbing on the east side of a long ridge. At mile 3, reach a small saddle before resuming the climb, now on the west side of the ridge. Watch for glimpses of Hillsboro Peak ahead.

At mile 3.6, continue straight at a four-way intersection, passing the Hillsboro Peak Bypass Trail No. 412. The trail swings to the south side of the peak, where snow may be found through late April, passing a faint trail to the right. Just below the peak at mile 4.8, bear left to stay on the Crest Trail, passing Trail No. 117 to Granite Peak. The large, flat area of the summit offers many good campsites, and the views from the fire lookout tower are especially fine in all directions. Hikers with only one vehicle may choose to return to the trailhead by the same route.

Continue west on the Crest Trail, now walking downhill and heading toward Board Gate Saddle. The Bypass Trail rejoins the Crest Trail at mile 5.2. The trail stays near the crest, crossing several saddles that offer scattered campsites as well as more views to the north and west. At mile 6.8, intersect the Railroad Canyon Trail No. 128 at a confusing intersection. Bear left onto the trail on the west side of the drainage, heading south and downhill. The trail follows the bottom of the drainage, making frequent crossings. At mile 8.7, intersect Trail No. 130. (The Emory Pass Trailhead can be reached via a strenuous climb on this trail.) Continue downstream, meeting the Gallina Canyon Trail No. 129 at mile 9.6. Bear left onto Trail No. 129 and continue to follow the stream, which below this point usually has running water. Cross the stream many times in the next mile, reaching Railroad Campground at mile 10.5.

Dipper tracks on rocks

SOURCES OF ADDITIONAL INFORMATION

National Parks and Monuments

Bandelier National Monument
HCR 1, Box 1, Suite 15
Los Alamos, NM 87544
(505) 672-0343
Chaco Culture NHP
Star Route 4, Box 6500
Bloomfield, NM 87413
(505) 786-7014
White Sands National Monument
P.O. Box 1086
Holloman Air Force Base, NM 88330
(505) 479-6124

Carlsbad Caverns National Park
3225 National Parks Highway
Carlsbad, NM 88220
(505) 785-2232
El Malpais National Monument
P.O. Box 939
Grants, NM 87020
(505) 285-4641

Bureau of Land Management

Albuquerque District Office
435 Montano Road NE
Albuquerque, NM 87107
(505) 761-8700
Farmington District Office
1235 La Plata Highway
Farmington, NM 87401
(505) 599-8900
Taos Resource Area
224 Cruz Alta
Taos, NM 87571
(505) 758-8851

El Malpais NCA
620 East Santa Fe Avenue
Grants, NM 87020
(505) 285-5406
Las Cruces District Office
1800 Marquess Street
Las Cruces, NM 88005
(505) 525-8228

Carson National Forest

Forest Supervisor
P.O. Box 558
Taos, NM 87571
(505) 758-6200
Camino Real Ranger District
P.O. Box 68
Peñasco, NM 87553
(505) 587-2255
Questa Ranger District
P.O. Box 110
Questa, NM 87556
(505) 586-0520

Canjilon Ranger District
P.O. Box 488
Canjilon, NM 87515
(505) 684-2486
El Rito Ranger District
P.O. Box 56
El Rito, NM 87530
(505) 581-4554
Tres Piedras Ranger District
P.O. Box 38
Tres Piedras, NM 87577
(505) 758-8678

Sources of Additional Information

Cibola National Forest

Forest Supervisor
2113 Osuna Road NE, Suite A
Albuquerque, NM 87113-1001
(505) 761-4650
Mount Taylor Ranger District
1800 Lobo Canyon Road
Grants, NM 87020
(505) 287-8833
Sandia Ranger District
Star Route, Box 174
Tijeras, NM 87059
(505) 281-3304

Magdalena Ranger District
P.O. Box 45
Magdalena, NM 87825
(505) 854-2281
Mountainair Ranger District
P.O. Box 69
Mountainair, NM 87036-0069
(505) 847-2990

Gila National Forest

Forest Supervisor
2610 North Silver Street
Silver City, NM 88061
(505) 388-8201
Glenwood Ranger District
P.O. Box 8
Glenwood, NM 88039
(505) 539-2481
Mimbres Ranger District
Route 11, Box 50
Mimbres, NM 88049
(505) 536-2250
Reserve Ranger District
P.O. Box 170
Reserve, NM 87830
(505) 533-6232
Wilderness Ranger District
Route 11, Box 50
Mimbres, NM 88049
(505) 536-2250

Black Range Ranger District
P.O. Box 431
Truth or Consequences, NM 87901
(505) 894-6677
Luna Ranger District
P.O. Box 91
Luna, NM 87824
(505) 547-2612
Quemado Ranger District
P.O. Box 158
Quemado, NM 87829
(505) 773-4678
Silver City Ranger District
2915 Highway 180 East
Silver City, NM 88061
(505) 538-2771

Lincoln National Forest

Forest Supervisor
1101 New York Avenue
Alamogordo, NM 88310-6992
(505) 437-6030
Guadalupe Ranger District
Federal Building, Room 159
Carlsbad, NM 88220
(505) 885-4181

Cloudcroft Ranger District
P.O. Box 288
Cloudcroft, NM 88317
(505) 682-2551
Smokey Bear Ranger District
901 Mechem Drive
Ruidoso, NM 88345
(505) 257-4095

Santa Fe National Forest

Forest Supervisor
P.O. Box 1689
Santa Fe, NM 87504
(505) 988-6940

Cuba Ranger District
P.O. Box 130
Cuba, NM 87013
(505) 289-3264

Jemez Ranger District
Jemez Springs District Office
Jemez Springs, NM 87025
(505) 829-3535

Coyote Ranger District
P.O. Box 160
Coyote, NM 87012
(505) 638-5526

Española Ranger District
P.O. Box R
Española, NM 87531
(505) 753-7331

Pecos Ranger District
P.O. Drawer 429
Pecos, NM 87552
(505) 757-6121

INDEX

About the Author

Born and raised in the suburbs of Philadelphia, Craig Martin fell in love with the mountains of New Mexico at the age of twelve when a fellow Boy Scout shared pictures of his trip to Philmont Scout Ranch near Cimarron. He has lived in New Mexico since 1987, exploring the state on foot, bike, cross-country skis, or with a fly rod in hand.

After working as a carpenter, a naturalist for the Delaware State Parks and the National Park Service, a geology instructor, and a junior high school science teacher, Martin took over primary care of his then-infant daughter and began a career as a freelance writer. He was editor of the award-winning *Fly-Fishing in Northern New Mexico* (The University of New Mexico Press, 1991) and its companion volume, *Fly Patterns for Northern New Mexico* (Sangre de Cristo Fly Fishers, 1992). He has also written three mountain bike guides including *Mountain Biking Northern New Mexico* (University of New Mexico Press, 1994), which features twenty-five tours into New Mexico's historical and geologic past. His writings have appeared in such magazines as *Sesame Street Parents, Delaware Conservationist, New Mexico Magazine, Fly Fisherman,* and *The Flyfisher.*

Martin lives in Los Alamos, New Mexico, with his wife, June, and children, Jessica and Alex, who all share his love of the outdoors.

Other books by The Mountaineers

If you enjoyed this book, you may also be interested in these related titles from The Mountaineers:

The *100 Hikes in*™ series:
Arizona by Scott S. Warren
California's Central Sierra & Coast Range by Vicky Spring
Colorado by Scott S. Warren
Inland Northwest by Rich Landers, Ida Rowe Dolphin
Northern California by John Soares, Marc Soares
Oregon by Rhonda Ostertag, George Ostertag
Washington's Alpine Lakes by Ira Spring, Vicky Spring, Harvey Manning
Washington's North Cascades: Glacier Peak Region by Ira Spring, Harvey Manning
Washington's North Cascades National Park Region by Ira Spring, Harvey Manning
Washington's South Cascades and Olympics by Ira Spring, Harvey Manning

Other regional titles:
Mountain Bike Adventures in the Four Corners Region by Michael McCoy
Hiking the Southwest's Canyon Country by Sandra Hinchman
Utah State Parks: A Complete Recreation Guide by Jan Bannan

THE MOUNTAINEERS, founded in 1906, is a nonprofit outdoor activity and conservation club, whose mission is "to explore, study, preserve, and enjoy the natural beauty of the outdoors. . . ." Based in Seattle, Washington, the club is now the third-largest such organization in the United States, with 15,000 members and four branches throughout Washington State.

The Mountaineers sponsors both classes and year-round outdoor activities in the Pacific Northwest, which include hiking, mountain climbing, ski-touring, snowshoeing, bicycling, camping, kayaking and canoeing, nature study, sailing, and adventure travel. The club's conservation division supports environmental causes through educational activities, sponsoring legislation, and presenting informational programs. All club activities are led by skilled, experienced volunteers, who are dedicated to promoting safe and responsible enjoyment and preservation of the outdoors.

The Mountaineers Books, an active, nonprofit publishing program of the club, produces guidebooks, instructional texts, historical works, natural history guides, and works on environmental conservation. All books produced by The Mountaineers are aimed at fulfilling the club's mission.

If you would like to participate in these organized outdoor activities or the club's programs, consider a membership in The Mountaineers. For information and an application, write or call The Mountaineers, Club Headquarters, 300 Third Avenue West, Seattle, Washington 98119; (206) 284-6310.

Send or call for our catalog of more than 300 outdoor titles:

 The Mountaineers Books
1001 SW Klickitat Way, Suite 201
Seattle, WA 98134
1-800-553-4453